How to Find GOD When You've Looked Everywhere

How to Find GOD When You've Looked Everywhere

Connecting with God
Abiding in God
Walking with God

W. Dee Kennedy

Bladensburg, MD

How To Find God When You've Looked Everywhere

Published by
Dove Christian Publishers
P.O. Box 611
Bladensburg, MD 20710-0611
www.dovechristianpublishers.com

Copyright © 2019 by W. Dee Kennedy

Cover Design by Mark Yearnings

All rights reserved. No part of this publication may be used or reproduced without permission of the publisher, except for brief quotes for scholarly use, reviews or articles.

Scripture quotations not notated are from the World English Bible (public domain)

Scriptures quotations marked KJV are from the King James Version of the Bible (public domain).

Scripture quotations taken from the New American Standard Bible® (NASB), Copyright © 1960, 1962, 1963, 1968, 1971, 1972, 1973, 1975, 1977, 1995 by The Lockman Foundation Used by permission. www.Lockman.org.

ISBN: 9781732112551

Printed in the United States of America

DEDICATION

Ami, Ann, Becky, Beth, Betty, Carl, Darcy, David, Deborah, Delbert, Dorothy, Elaine, Ellen, Ellie, Gail, George, Georgia, Hannah, Heather, Jane, James, Jeremy, Jim, John, Joya, Leonard, Marjory, Mikayla, Nancy, Pat, Rex, Robert, Shelley, Vern, Vin, Yvonne.

In all of these people, I have seen the glory of God. I know them.

Contents

Preface	vii
Introduction	xi
Chapter 1	
God Wants To Be Found	1
Chapter 2	
How God Finds Us	17
Chapter 3	
How To Connect To God	34
Chapter 4	
What It's Like To Get Closer To God	54
Chapter 5	
Getting Closer To God Through Worship	80
Chapter 6	
The Cleansing Relationship	106
Chapter 7	
Some People Just Don't Want To Find God	132
Notes	146

PREFACE

It may seem unusual for a mechanical engineer to write a book about Christian spirituality. The reasoning of the engineer may seem a million miles away from the righteousness of God. My career in construction required that I install mechanical systems into modern buildings. My task as a writer involves knowledge of the things of God. How did I go from one kind of logic to the other?

As I have now discovered, the two kinds of knowledge, mechanical and spiritual, are closer than I had once imagined. God's logic can be sequential, like mechanical logic, or non-sequential. Some may regard God's non-sequential logic as "circular." A more accurate term, however, is "spherical" because of its multi-dimensional and comprehensive quality. In both areas (mechanical and spiritual), truth is orderly and can be proved. If anyone cannot discern God's logic clearly, it may be because they understand neither his starting nor his ending points. If we guess at God's methods, purposes, and goals using our human logic, we may decide what God would do based on what we might do—or again, based on what we have been taught. Because of this limited perspective, our logical inferences about God become clumsy, from start to finish, and we stumble.

The path of conventional religious opinion caused me to stumble once, as many others have done. At an early age, I followed God as best I logically could, in linear and sequential ways, just as I had been taught. The people around me appeared to do the same. I approached spirituality rationally and practically. I attended church, read the Bible, and prayed because those practices were socially respectable and condoned. The Lord blessed my efforts. I was on the right path, so I thought; the path of a self-directed life.

In my early fifties, this rational and practical path came to an end. Now, at this juncture, I have become acquainted with God's non-sequential ways—the spherical reasoning of God, if you will. Although the linear and conventional path to God had taken me a long way, now I could walk no farther. Confused and discouraged, I experimented with many things to find my way over this roadblock. Nothing worked. Finally, I stopped trying altogether. I quit church, Bible study, and prayer. I told the Lord that I would wait on him to show me the way forward since, by my own efforts, I had hit an impasse. Over ten years elapsed while I waited without receiving a clear response from God. I had forgotten my prayer once the answer finally came.

The Lord found me, got my attention, and made me aware of different paths in which to walk: the paths of the God-directed life, as Jeremiah describes.

> *Stand in the ways and see, and ask for the old paths, 'Where is the good way?' and walk in it, and you will find rest for your souls (Jeremiah 6:16)*

The ancient and good way extended before me. Only with his hand to lead me could I make the leap from a self-directed life to a God-directed one.

This book describes the methods that I discovered for following the life-giving paths of a God-directed life. These paths have led me out of darkness into the light. The future is now unlimited. I had to relearn God's desires and will for my life. I found different ways to connect with God, to abide in God, and to walk with God. I offer this book in the hope that what I have learned may assist others who seek a spiritual path forward.

INTRODUCTION

There must be thousands of books about God's righteousness and his will for our lives. Such books keep getting written and read because God's people everywhere keep searching for answers that directly satisfy their hearts. God invites us to be with him and to walk in his ways. While this invitation drives us to keep studying his Word, much confusion prevails as to how to do so. Thousands of voices clamor for attention on this subject. Various churches, preachers, or gurus–and assorted zealots or non-believers (as the case may be)—shout out their different versions of the truth. Each of us is responsible for what we shall believe.

We may become rich in the knowledge of sacred and secular subjects–including the Bible, theology, and ecclesiastical history on the one hand, and philosophy or the sciences on the other. None of this human knowledge, however valuable, can directly feed us spiritually or give us access to God. Neither our friends nor our church experience, neither this book nor any other book, can substitute for a spiritual awareness of God. We must each hear the voice of the Holy Spirit for ourselves and respond in our own way. The Holy Spirit communicates through love and by the heart, rather than through the mind and by rational knowledge. This contact with the Spirit of God is an experience we need and long for. Theoretical knowledge can never substitute for the touch of God—which is tender yet powerful.

The paths of righteousness are not confined to some particular church or holy place, nor are they laid out merely by doctrines or creeds. Our Lord has sheep in every church, and many of his favored ones are not attending any formal church or any congregation at all. Many of His would-be followers have not yet heard his invitation.

I hope that through this book, God's invitation will be heard by spiritual seekers, whether they be Christian or religiously unaffiliated. While my book deals with the biblical revelation of God through Jesus Christ, my style is non-dogmatic. I discuss universal spiritual experiences—such as love, forgiveness, sin, and truth—rather than confining my attention to parochial matters or in-house theological debates.

The book describes three unique relationships we may have with God through Jesus Christ. The first is the *saving relationship* through which we first connect with God. The second is the *abiding relationship*. Here, we become one with him. The third is the *cleansing relationship*. With this we are cleansed of the tendencies to wrongdoing we have protected and maintained all of our lives. As we learn about and take part in these relationships, we embark upon a God-directed life. This new life will become instinctive.

While this book includes readings of the Bible and theological reasoning, it should inspire curiosity and receptivity to spiritual things rather than to coerce assent to doctrinal or philosophical arguments. The aim is not to add to one's intellectual knowledge, primarily. This book will succeed if one's heart comes alive by the Holy Spirit.

> *He restoreth my soul. He leads me in the paths of righteousness for his namesake (Psalms 23:3).*

CHAPTER *1*

GOD WANTS TO BE FOUND

In the beginning, God created the heavens and the earth. The earth was formless and empty. Darkness was on the surface of the deep and God's Spirit was hovering over the surface of the waters. God said, "Let there be light," and there was light. God saw the light, and saw that it was good. God divided the light from the darkness. God called the light "day," and the darkness he called "night." There was evening and there was morning, the first day (Genesis 1:1-5)

If we read the Bible as a whole from a Christian perspective, then the end is contained in the beginning. The New Testament affirms that God is love. With this affirmation, we may then read the first chapter of the Bible. God's creation begins the greatest love story ever told. Our Lord created this world, saying "it was good" (Genesis 1:31). Out of love for the people of his creation, God offered good things. The best thing of all is for us to receive God's love and to love him in return.

Creating this world was not a mere experiment on God's part nor a trial as if just a practice session for the next big thing. Not an experiment (which might go wrong), the universe became a home for the most complex creatures ever made: man and woman. God made the people of this world so they could think, reason, and have opinions. We were built with free will and the power of choice. God made us people who share in his creativity. We make and create things. We were made to give and receive love, both in relation to God and each other. We were made in God's image (Genesis 1:26).

This new earth would be a perfect home for God's creation. Designed to make us comfortable and provide for our every need, the earth was beautiful to behold. Everything was alive. This world would be self-sustaining in order to receive and support the population that would become the offspring of the first couple, Adam and Eve. Through it all, the new people made by God would share love with each other and with the Creator of all things. The God of love desires to share his good creation with human beings.

People who wish to be connected with God must do so through the bond of love. Love will be in our hearts as surely as the love that binds us to our friends, our children, and our spouses. Love is a mystery, difficult to describe. Our love for others can only be understood through an experiential understanding. Love for God, similarly, involves experience and intuition. Everything we know, or think we know about God must begin from the affirmation that God is love. The New Testament sings of God's love:

God is love, and he who remains in love remains in God, and God remains in him (1 John 4:16).

We love him, because he first loved us (1 John 4:19).

All love that we have in our hearts is from God. There is no other source, for God is love itself. He created love inside of us as certainly as he created the world in which we live.

LIGHT AND DARKNESS

The first verses of Genesis describe the first day of creation. What a day it was! Even though the sun and moon were not created on the first day, there was light. The light described is the divine light, a source that goes beyond created sources of light (e.g., planetary bodies) in physical or material terms. Since the sun and moon were not put in place until the fourth day of creation, the light existing on the first day came directly from God. As the New Testament affirms:

God is light, and in him is no darkness at all (1 John 1:5).

By creating light on the first day of creation, God announced both his presence and his authority. The dividing line between daylight and darkness distinguished light and darkness in the naturalistic and physical sense. Darkness became the absence of light. Symbolically and metaphysically, light and darkness signify good and evil, respectively. This first act of God demonstrated that God's very nature is to be the light as the New Testament states (John 1:4). Those who wanted to be part of his kingdom longed for the light and move to the light. Those who did not want to be part of his kingdom would stay in darkness and move away from the light. There would be people in the new world, created by God, who would choose the darkness rather than the light.

From the start, God in God's omniscience knew that some would choose darkness. God prepared for that refusal. His people had free will, and he knew many would not come to the light. The Book of Revelation describes the future kingdom on earth, which is made new, as having no night (Revelation

21:25). When there is no darkness, in the new kingdom, there is no evil.

No one can know why some people choose evil and stay away from the light. However, he gives us the choice to stay in the darkness away from him. God wants to be surrounded by people who truly love and want to be with him. For this freedom to be preserved, they must have the ability to say no. Love, according to God's definition, depends on free will and cannot be forced.

> *For only love can satisfy love, and love cannot be compelled! To win a person's friendship, you clasp his hand — you do not clench your fist. All genuine affection springs from free volition, and you cannot truly love without the power to choose. (W. Ian Thomas)*[1]

Freedom sets the stage for potential conflicts, since some choose light and others darkness. As a result of this conflict between light and darkness, God the Father, through his only begotten Son, is on a mission to eliminate the darkness. By establishing a kingdom based on love, which will last without sin for all eternity, God aims to gather a people who want him to be their God; they want to be his people. The people of his kingdom leave the darkness for the kingdom of the light.

Before we can understand our Lord's vision for the lives of his people, we must have a good understanding of his desires from the very beginning.

GOD WANTS A PEOPLE TO SHARE HIS LOVE

Since love works through relationships, God seeks to establish a connection and relationship with each person. By revealing himself to us, God invites us to come and join with him. Those who hear and accept this invitation come into the light. They become God's people of the light. He wants *all* who will to join him, "that they may have life, and may have it abundantly" (John 10:10).

If God's people cannot choose against him, they cannot truly love him in the way God desires, for they cannot be his friends. The kingdom is to comprise his friends, not his servants. The New Testament states this message through Jesus Christ, who is sent by God.

> *No longer do I call you servants, for the servant doesn't know what his lord does. But I have called you friends, for everything that I heard from my Father, I have made known to you (John 15:15).*

Eleven of Jesus' disciples had the privilege of hearing these words in person, from Jesus' own lips. This verse comes from the farewell discourse in the Gospel of John, which contains final instructions to the disciples just a few hours before Jesus' arrest. Less than twenty-four hours after delivering these instructions, Jesus will have died and been lying in the tomb. The farewell discourse, recorded in the Gospel of John (chapters 13 through 17), may be the most poignant, intimate, and powerful talk of Jesus' ministry on earth. All who receive the words from this speech will be blessed. Jesus is speaking not just to his designated disciples but also to his friends and to all who read the gospel in later generations.

This final talk may address us personally if we listen with our hearts, as if we were being addressed directly and individually. Each of us is a friend of the Lord, who has something to tell us —

each of us, personally.

Let us think of our own friends, how many of them come and go, how few stay in our lives forever. In fact, friendship is special because, while a friend has the freedom to walk away, he or she stays and loves through thick or thin, in good times or bad, amidst rough times or smooth. Only the full commitment of friendship provides an honest and equal connection, from heart to heart, upon which a true relationship is built. Friends exchange ideas, back and forth, while listening and responding to each other. Friends respect each other, while exploring ideas, learning together, and loving. Such a relationship benefits both people in the partnership and those in their social circle.

Many couples form the mutually beneficial relationships John describes. These couples maintain a bond that is loving, affirming, and nurturing. Their sharing with each other is amazing to experience, just as Jesus desires. The marriage relationship, while different from friendship, is strengthened by friendship and God's love:

> *He answered, "Haven't you read that he who made them from the beginning made them male and female, and said, 'For this cause a man shall leave his father and mother, and shall join to his wife; and the two shall become one flesh?' So that they are no more two, but one flesh. What therefore God has joined together, don't let man tear apart"* (Matthew 19:4-6).

In the divine scheme, marriage is as close to a perfect relationship as one can have in our lives. Marriage is a model of the relationship Jesus desires with each one of us. We are to become one with him as husband and wife are one: "no more two, but one flesh" (Matthew 19:6). Similarly, Jesus prays for unity among his disciples:

> *That they may all be one; even as you, Father, are in me, and I in you, that they also may be one in us; that the world may believe that you sent me (John 17:21).*

Most couples do not achieve an ideal of total oneness. Not even the followers of Jesus will be capable of total oneness with him on this earth. But we should not get discouraged. He wants the relationship between himself and each of us to begin in this world while extending into the world to come. A whole eternity stretches out in which we may grow closer to God. Love does not change. Love is timeless.

We usually focus on what our Lord is doing for us and what we are receiving from God. However, God asks for something from us. Beyond the gifts of God, such as life, love, salvation, acceptance, and eternal life, God seeks a relationship with us, which entails mutuality. Relationships are about both parties. Both contribute and receive benefits, one from the other. Yes, God wants to receive benefit from us: our love, freely given.

> *In the beginning was the Word, and the Word was with God, and the Word was God. The same was in the beginning with God. All things were made through him. Without him was not anything made that has been made. In him was life, and the life was the light of men. The light shines in the darkness, and the darkness hasn't overcome it (John 1:1-5).*

We serve an incredible creator God. "It is he that hath made us, and not we ourselves" (Psalm 100:3). Having created this wonderful world in which we live, God created Adam and Eve to share his creativity. He left it to us to procreate and give birth to the rest of humanity. We share in this divine creative power. God created the people of earth with special endowments:

- We are given dominion over the earth.
- We have the ability to reproduce.
- We have the ability to think and to act and to accomplish.
- We are created to be in the image of God.

Wonderful things indeed! We are special because God made and loves us. Each of us must decide how we should live our lives and how we will fit into this world in which we live. The creator God is all about love. So, our lives are intended to be fulfilled (and fulfilling). Our joy is to be full. This universe is to be filled with people with whom to share God's love. We as human beings are to be with God forever as Jesus explains:

I am going to prepare a place for you. If I go and prepare a place for you, I will come again, and will receive you to myself; that where I am, you may be there also (John 14:2-3).

God did not create robots or even servants. We are created as friends, friends according to our free will. Genuine friends can stop loving if they choose to so, but they will never make that choice. Such a community of friends may seem like an impossible accomplishment. With God all things are possible.

God has a plan so that we will be knit together in bonds of friendship. For our own benefit, God's dealings with us are as transparent as possible because God operates on the principle of full disclosure. His covenant with us is completely open. We receive this disclosure through a written record (the Bible) which has been passed down through the ages. Of course, God's first plan started in the garden with Adam and Eve. They met with God daily. They learned from him face to face. There was no death, no separation. Later, separation ensued, a separation that God wants to mend so we might reconnect with him and more deeply love him again.

GOD'S CHANGING WAYS TO CONNECT WITH HIS PEOPLE

When Adam and Eve were initially in the garden, they were connected to God and walked with him. Their ways were the same, the divine and the human. As they matured, they developed doubts about God's leadership and authority. They must have been wondering whether all of his guidance was in their best interest. When the couple ate from the tree which had been forbidden, they broke the relationship of trust. They chose their way over God's way.

Everything changed. Adam and Eve also changed. They had lost their natural connection with God. They became separated from him. Their children would now be born without this special connection as well. They no longer had access to their garden home. They had to begin again in a less protected environment outside the garden of Eden.

Both God and the couple recognized the loss and God developed a plan of restoration. A special representative would be sent to enable a new union of humankind with God. This man would be a peacemaker, a mediator, specially appointed to reconcile the relationship that had been lost between humanity and God. Once they heard this new message of hope, the descendants of Adam and Eve (who constituted God's people) longed for the day of its coming. Throughout the history of Israel, God and his people were bound in a covenant. However, evil continued to abound. The prophets glimpsed the coming of this appointed messiah and Savior whom God had ordained and set apart for a holy mission.

Once this messenger was sent by God, as the New Testament recounts, the story of Jesus Christ—and God's love—spread entirely by personal testimony. During this period many people heard Christ's invitation for reconciliation with God and they came into the light. Seeking a restored relationship with God, they chose the ways that Christ set out for them.

The history of Israel may be divided into epochs. The first epoch lasts from Adam to Abraham. The light was almost overtaken by the darkness during this time. But God and his people endured through the strife of Cain and Abel, the devastation of the flood, and the wreckage left after Babel. Righteous men like Noah and many others were approved by God. The light continued. Then, God changed his approach to humanity because humanity had changed. While tribalism and city-states were fading, nations were being formed. International trade began on a large scale. God's goal remained the same: that people might know him and come into the light. He developed a different method to achieve this goal. His people would carry his message, as a nation among other nations.

God formalized religion while the Jewish nation took shape, a process that took five-hundred years beginning with the birth of Abraham in what is now eastern Iraq. Abraham and Sarah moved into the land promised to them in Canaan, which lies along the Jordan River. From Canaan, his people moved into Egypt. Five hundred years after the birth of Abraham, a million and a half Israelites walked out of Egypt at the time of the exodus. Struggling in the desert, they crossed the Jordan river back into Canaan after forty years. Now they were carrying their tabernacle, their teachings, and their traditions. Thereupon they occupied the promised land promised to Abraham 500 years before. Jerusalem became the capital and the center of worship. Schools were started. A nation was born. People continued to hear God's invitation and come into the light.

After more than a millennium (about 1,500 years later), our Lord changed his approach to humanity once again, because humanity had changed. The same goal remained in place as in the garden. A different method would be required. God did not change, nor his goal; only the means to accomplish the goal. Now, God incarnated in Jesus Christ and came to earth himself. Having taken on human form, God through Jesus Christ fulfilled the law that had not been kept by human beings. He became the mediator between God and humanity, the one who could stand between the two and reconcile their differences.

After the time of Jesus, religious institutions became decentralized. This context meant that the message of the gospel could spread and multiply throughout the world. Jerusalem was no longer the center of worship. The blood sacrifice of animals stopped, a system that had been in place for four thousand years.

The priesthood of all believers was established, entailing a new set of beliefs and practices, namely:

- Faith in Jesus as the Son of God
- Repentance
- Baptism by the Holy Spirit

God's people quickly started to meet in groups. These congregations were called churches. God's people spread over the earth, having heard the invitation from God through Jesus Christ. They came into the light, having chosen God's way.

Some believe that the previous approaches of God toward his people failed. However, we can think of such perceived failures differently. Every approach by God to draw humanity to himself has been successful. Each approach by the divine has been built on the foundation of the preceding ones. Millions of adherents have come to the light, no matter the approach. His methods of drawing human beings to himself have been adapted to the particular circumstances in each era. God's ways always meet our needs, and when our needs are met, his needs and goals are met. God is a servant God.

Here is the Old Testament plan, a covenant which puts God in relationship with his people:

> *But this is the covenant that I will make with the house of Israel after those days, says Yahweh: I will put my law in their inward parts, and in their heart will I write it; and I will be their God, and they shall be my people (Jeremiah 31:33).*

> *I will walk among you, and will be your God, and you will be my people (Leviticus 26:12).*

Here is the New Testament plan:

> *For you are a temple of the living God. Even as God said, "I will dwell in them, and walk in them; and I will be their God, and they will be my people" (2 Corinthians 6:16).*

> *"For this is the covenant that I will make with the house of Israel. After those days," says the Lord; I will put my laws into their mind. I will also write them on their heart. I will be their God, and they will be my people" (Hebrews 8:10).*

Here is the plan for the new earth, after the kingdom of God is established:

> *I heard a loud voice out of heaven saying, "Behold, God's dwelling is with people, and he will dwell with them, and they will be his people, and God himself will be with them as their God" (Revelation 21:3).*

These scriptures reflect what God wanted for his people at different stages in salvation history, from the pre-flood world until today. God's purposes are consistent for each epoch depending on circumstances: for the kingdom of Israel (in the past), for his people here today (in the present), and for the new earth (in the coming epoch). God is to be our God, and we are his people. The goals of God, to love and be bound to us in relationship, are achieved–in the past, present, and for the future.

GOD'S PEOPLE RESPOND TO HIM

While we live on this earth, God invites us to be a part of his plan. The invitation is open for those with ears to hear his divine voice. Those who hear the invitation can respond. He has given this same invitation from the beginning of history.

> *By faith, Abel offered to God a more excellent sacrifice than Cain, through which he had testimony given to him that he was righteous, God testifying with respect to his gifts; and through it he, being dead, still speaks (Hebrews 11:4).*

Abel heard the voice of the Lord, believed it, and responded. He obeyed God. This obedience was counted to him as righteousness.

By faith, Enoch was taken away, so that he wouldn't see death, and he was not found, because God translated him. For he has had testimony given to him that before his translation he had been well pleasing to God (Hebrews 11:5).

Enoch listened to God and followed the divine ways. This obedience was counted to Enoch as righteousness.

By faith, Noah, being warned about things not yet seen, moved with godly fear, prepared a ship for the saving of his house, through which he condemned the world, and became heir of the righteousness which is according to faith (Hebrews 11:7).

Noah heard God, believed him, and acted on his belief. This act of faith was counted to him as righteousness.

And what is faith?

Now faith is assurance of things hoped for, proof of things not seen (Hebrews 11:1).

What about Abraham? God had promised Abraham that he would be the progenitor of a nation of many. However, Abraham was desperate when, at seventy years old, he still had no heir. He talked to God about this problem. He thought that Eliezer, his lead employee, would be his heir.

Behold, Yahweh's word came to him, saying, "This man will not be your heir, but he who will come out of your own body will be your heir." Yahweh brought him outside, and said, "Look now toward the sky, and count the stars, if you are able to count them." He said to Abram, "So will your offspring be." He believed in Yahweh, who credited it to him for righteousness (Genesis 15:4-6).

Abraham heard the word of the Lord and believed him, and it

was counted to him as righteousness.

Sarah stands out as unique in the list of the faithful, given in Hebrews 11. Sarah has a fascinating history (Genesis 16:1-10). Abraham told her about God's promise of not only bearing a son, but that she would also have children as numerous as the stars in the heavens. Some fifteen years later, considering the matter logically, Sarah became impatient with waiting for God to act. She took matters into her own hands. She told Abraham that there was no way she could have children because of her age. So, she provided her handmaid to him as a wife so he might have natural children.

Sarah's strategy for giving Abraham a son didn't work out well. Our personal strategies to do God's will often fail when we take things into our own hands. Her handmaid, Hagar, gave birth to Ishmael and the strife in Sarah's tent never stopped. Finally, Hagar ran away from the camp. The Lord brought her back, and she learned to live with Sarah.

Abraham was eighty-five when Ishmael was born. Abraham was ninety-nine when the promise was repeated for the last time. Sarah was included, specifically by name this time. Angels visited Abraham and repeated the promise a third time (Genesis 18:9-15). Abraham learned that the promise would happen within a year. Sarah was listening from the tent during this conversation. She could hear every word. Sarah laughed when Abraham was told that his wife would be pregnant in a few short months.

In the biblical story, God hears her laughter in the tent and rebukes her. Sarah denies laughing. God says, "Yes, you did" (Genesis 18:15), which is a second rebuke. This final rebuke was what Sarah seemed to need. She finally gets the point. She accepts God's word.

She gives up her own judgments and believes what God has told her. Within a few months, she is pregnant. What does the scripture say about Sarah?

> *By faith, even Sarah herself received power to conceive, and she bore a child when she was past age, since she counted him faithful who had promised. Therefore as many as the stars of the sky in multitude, and as innumerable as the sand which is by the sea shore, were fathered by one man, and him as good as dead (Hebrews 11:11-12).*

These followers of God had one thing in common. They could hear their Master. He called them by name, and they followed him. They heard his voice—they believed—and acted on their belief. Then, it was counted to them as righteousness.

In Eden, at the time of the flood, and after the flood until today, the principles of faith are constant. After the cross, similarly, our belief in God's word is counted to us as righteousness.

CHAPTER 2

HOW GOD FINDS US

This chapter will illustrate the methods that Jesus uses to bring his disciples to faith by examining three significant biblical passages. Jesus meets a Samaritan woman at a well. By teaching her with compassion, he leads her to joy and faith. Similarly, in an extended dialogue with a man named Nicodemus, Jesus guides this ruler of the Jews to a point of decision about matters of faith. Once again, in a message to Laodicea in the Book of Revelation, the personal and dialogical style of Jesus' teaching is displayed. Jesus' method of intimate conversation and conversion to faith is still in operation today. Jesus brings all who hear his voice to a decision point. Each of his listeners must respond of his or her own free will. Each must discern the Spirit. The decision that one makes–or fails to make–will bring about a complete change of life.

These three figures—the Samaritan Woman, Nicodemus, and the Laodiceans—represent three of the many kinds of people with whom Jesus spoke and interacted while on his earthly mission. They all needed to unite with him as true disciples, but their histories and experiences were all completely different. Jesus could not overpower their thinking about what they believed on their own. They had to "hear his voice" and to have "ears to hear and eyes to see" (Mark 4:9). Only then could they meet the criteria of salvation. They had to personally recognize the "voice" of God while responding to his invitation.

When talking to others about religion, it doesn't take much time to discover spiritual differences. The situation is the same now as it was in the time of Jesus. Human nature has not changed. Each individual's personal spirituality is deeply held; thus, our very core is shaken when our beliefs are challenged. We perceive that our personal identity is at stake. We become hesitant to share our feelings or even to ask questions. The results can be unsettling since we want to feel safe. These feelings are so strong that friendships can end over differences in spiritual beliefs. Groups of people, even families, can be divided. Churches will split into factions.

Jesus faces the risk of challenging another's belief in every person he met, both during the time of his historical ministry and today. Jesus reveals himself to every person, every day. How does he address all people so they may overcome their deeply held prejudices and recognize the truth he longs to share? His conversations with three representative believers–the woman of Samaria, Nicodemus, and the church of Laodicea—show a similar method of dialogue, a method he still continues to use today.

HIS METHOD DISPLAYED

The Samaritan Woman

The day was too warm. Sweat was running down his legs, mixing with the dust of the road he and his companions had been traveling. The sun was overhead. He sat on the stones that had been laid around the famous well, amid the land that was called Samaria. Jesus was thirsty. He and his group had been traveling for three or four days from the Jordan River area near Jericho, where they had been preaching and baptizing (John 4:1-6).

The trip had been difficult. It had started more than 800 ft. below sea level and had taken them to Sychar, a Samaritan town 1,800 feet above sea level near Jacob's Well. The trip had been over forty miles. We don't know the route they traveled, but the climb out of the Jordan Valley is difficult at any location.

His disciples had gone on to the town to buy food while he sat at the well alone and waited for his appointment. Yes, the same Lord who saw Nathanael under the fig tree before Philip found him must have known about the unnamed woman, who was carrying her pitcher and making her way to the well. The woman would pass the disciples of Jesus, who were going in the opposite direction. They were headed into the town, and she was going to the well to draw water as part of her daily routine (John 4:7-26). The Samaritan woman didn't know that she would become a part of the next appointment with Jesus. She had a troubled heart, which Jesus knew well.

Even a casual observer might have perceived this woman's desolation or her burden of problems. Instead of joining the group of women, who used to go to the well together, she was by herself at noon. This time of day would normally be the least likely time to find someone drawing water from a well. The correct time of day to get water from the well was typically late afternoon when the sun hung low in the sky. The women of the village would travel together to draw and transport water, a shared activity. They would talk about the happenings of the day and share the normal social gossip among them as people have done to this day.

That the woman had five husbands—while she was now living

with another man to whom she was not married—ensured that the solitary woman, who was heading toward the well at noon, would become the object of gossip in the small town. She did not care to listen to the conversation about her behavior: neither the criticisms by neighbors nor their many repeated stories. Some women would speak things about her out of her hearing; others would speak audibly. There may have been women who held a personal grudge against her. She could not bear their talk. The Samaritan woman knew that she was not doing everything right; she had a problem, but she felt helpless. Her emotional pain, held inside, isolated her, though she kept looking for relief.

The Samaritan woman silently passed the disciples on their way to buy food. More Jews, she thought. Jews were always traveling through her village, back and forth, on the main road between Galilee and Jerusalem. *Why do they think themselves better than us Samaritans?* She reflected. *I don't understand why they believe their religion to be superior. At least our village can sell them food and make money from them!*

The sight of a single Jewish man, at the well by himself, must have looked strange. Why did he linger and not go along with the others? Why was he alone? The man looked harmless enough, even kind. She got her water as usual and remain silent as custom dictated. After collecting her water quickly, she would depart just as fast. What happened next changed her life and changed the world.

This meeting at the well was one of the most extended private conversations that Jesus held. The Samaritan woman had questions about her spiritual life. She wanted to know if the religion of her people was adequate and if she was "safe," spiritually. Although she believed in the coming of the Messiah, she did not understand personal righteousness.

Nicodemus

Jesus spoke at length, privately, not only with the Samaritan woman but also with Nicodemus. These two significant dialogues display his personal approach when faced with would-be believers who are initially reluctant and who even strongly question his message. Both discussions demonstrate his love for the person with whom he is speaking and his desire for a deeper level of intimacy. Jesus wants to connect at the heart level with both the Samaritan woman and Nicodemus. In doing so, he brings them to a decision point. However, he tailored his message for each to fit their individual differences. He presents the same message in two different ways.

Nicodemus was a leader of great stature and a member of the Pharisees (John 3:1-21). He came to Jesus by night with questions. He could not dare to risk his reputation by being seen in the private company of a rabbi, Jesus of Nazareth, who had caused such problems for the Jewish leadership. All the Pharisees hated Jesus. However, Nicodemus could not help but meet with him. It must have felt like a strange compulsion for this leader of the Jews, for Nicodemus had serious questions.

Nicodemus did not comprehend the difference between faith and works, nor did he understand the nature of real faith. He had always achieved righteousness by keeping the law, just as he had been taught while growing up and in his training as a teacher of the law. Since he heard and saw Jesus, Nicodemus had questioned his understanding of the Messiah's nature and mission. While

Nicodemus had a good understanding of the need for a correct standing before God, just as any teacher of the Pharisees would, he believed he lacked this and didn't know how to get it. He had no idea what would happen when Jesus found him.

Laodicea

Laodicea was a city in ancient Asia Minor. Paul spoke of it several times. An early Christian church could be found there only miles from the city of Colossae. This city was the same that Paul mentions in his letter to the Colossians (Colossians 2:1). This Laodicean church was among the seven churches addressed in the Book of Revelation, found in Revelation 3:14-20.

The Laodicean church members had been baptized into the New Testament church. They had all the forms of the New Testament religion but none of its power. Covering themselves with the protection of wealth and knowledge, they believed that they had "need of nothing" (Revelation 3:17). They did not understand how to connect with God, nor even the need of it. They were quite satisfied to be left alone. They had an intellectual understanding of God, but their hearts had no understanding.

STEP ONE: *GET OUR ATTENTION*

In Jesus' method of dialogue, his first words aimed to get people's attention. This first step is taught to all public speakers. The listeners need to stop letting their minds wander among their distractions (i.e., whatever topics are absorbing their current thoughts) in order to focus on the speaker's words. The speaker has something important to impart to hearers. His first words invite them to listen to what he is about to say.

The Samaritan Woman

To the Samaritan woman, Jesus said, "Give me a drink of water" (John 4:7). These words are all that was needed. In today's world, the request may not seem remarkable, but in the historical moment and culture, the words were unheard of. The request of a drink from a Jewish man got the attention of the Samaritan woman because Jews and Samaritans never talked to one another. It wasn't done. During this shocking encounter, Jesus dared to speak to the woman of Samaria, and he instantly had her rapt attention. That she answered him back let him know that this woman was ready for the next step. A "proper" Samaritan woman would have kept quiet, even when spoken to by a Jew. Quietly, she would have drawn her water and left. Her boldness to give him her attention indicates a readiness to learn more from this Jewish teacher.

Nicodemus

Jesus invited Nicodemus to discipleship by the bold claim: "You must be born again" (John 3:3). The circumstances of their meeting were shrouded as if they were shameful. Having initiated the interview, Nicodemus came to Jesus at night, so as not to take the chance of being discovered with the controversial Jewish rabbi. His reputation in the community could be jeopardized.

Nicodemus began the conversation by making observations about the ministry of Jesus and its power, perhaps to flatter the so-called prophet. Jesus would have none of it. Jesus would not let him lead this meeting, for he already knew the needs and motivations of Nicodemus. Cutting immediately to the heart of the matter, Jesus declared, "You must be born again" (John 3:3). At this,

Nicodemus lost his composure and betrayed his ignorance about the Messiah's mission and purpose. Now that Jesus had his full attention, Nicodemus was ready to listen.

Laodiceans

Concerning the Laodiceans, Jesus condemns their lukewarm behavior, warning that he would spew them out of his mouth. Several biblical translations use the word "vomit." This graphic word is strong language and makes as potent an impact as the phrase of the Apostle Paul when he labeled the Corinthians as "people of the flesh, babies in Christ" (1 Cor. 3:1). Christ speaks harshly so that the Laodiceans may open their ears and hear his message, just as Paul wrote with striking imagery to the Corinthians. Their behavior has shown him that they are not remembering with gratitude how they have been blessed in the past and what their journey as his people should be like. Paul, in the same manner, wanted to wake up the Corinthians.

Will these words get the attention of the Laodiceans? Time will tell. Will they listen? They will if they "have ears to hear." In chapter seven, the identity of the Laodiceans will become clear. It will be up to each member of the Laodicean church to pay attention, hear the divine message, and respond. Each must do so alone. No one can help someone "hear" the message of God.

STEP TWO: *TURN OUR THINKING UPSIDE DOWN*

Even after our attention is focused on Jesus, the path to the heart may remain blocked. We may be suspicious. Our minds are often determined to maintain the status quo of our lives. We resist change. We barricade ourselves with many biases. We surround ourselves with friends that believe the same as we do. Too many things press upon us, and we avoid change, even if the change might initially seem to be positive. Comfortable with our current problems and reluctant to trade them away for the unknown, we shrink from the complexities that any profound life change may likely entail. It requires much effort to dismantle the seemingly "safe" place we have established for ourselves.

All life changes can be difficult. Think about the changes required during various life transitions, such as a house purchase and mortgage, a marriage, a new job, a move, a pregnancy, or a death in the family. Such complex changes involve lots of unknown factors. We rarely gravitate toward the unknown in our lives.

These human habits and psychological processes were obvious in each person who Jesus met. The same is true today. Once Jesus gains the attention of his listeners and dialogue partners, he can prepare them for a change of thought and heart. But their free decision has to be respected. In his effort to get them to open to a new spiritual awareness, Jesus turns logic as if "upside down." Many people have relied on the logic of traditional teaching and popular opinion. God's logic can differ greatly from ours and may seem inverted ("upside down") when heard for the first time. Listeners must reconsider long-held spiritual beliefs without becoming defensive or entering into petty arguments.

The Samaritan Woman

Jesus got the attention of the woman at the well by alerting her that she was in the presence of someone special who could give her "living" water. When she heard this new thought, she immediately engaged in the conversation. They spoke back and forth. She even ridiculed his assertions. Jesus continued to speak of the wonderful water that would spring up within her into everlasting life. As she was convinced, the Samaritan woman opened her mind to other possibilities. Now she was ready to listen and absorb whatever came next.

Nicodemus

Nicodemus came to Jesus to get answers to the questions that had occupied his mind since he had first witnessed Jesus and heard the gospel. After Nicodemus put his attention in the right place, Jesus turned his thinking upside down. The Lord treated him similarly as Nicodemus might have treated one of his own students. Because Nicodemus was a teacher of duty (and responsibility to the law), he should have understood what he was hearing. Jesus even corrected him for his lack of understanding.

> *Most certainly I tell you, we speak that which we know, and testify of that which we have seen, and you don't receive our witness (John 3:11).*

Jesus and the prophets had been telling the Jewish nation the truth, which they had refused to accept. After being corrected a second time, Nicodemus hears what Jesus says. He accepts and follows.

> *If I told you earthly things and you don't believe, how will you believe if I tell you heavenly things? (John 3:12)*

Out of love, Jesus corrected all those with whom he walked on earth, as many examples in the four Gospels show. He often corrected his apostles so they would learn the proper way to live and think, as God intends. Parents today raise their children by correcting them endlessly. Once Jesus returned to heaven after his resurrection, the Holy Spirit took over the role of correcting God's people and does so today—again, because of God's love. He only corrects the people who have chosen to become his sons and daughters.

Nicodemus continued to awaken during his dialogue with Jesus. Jesus taught him that reliance on the flesh (works) is meaningless. He could not achieve righteousness on his own. Only the Spirit can affect this kind of change in a person. The keeping of the law by obedience to the writings of man is never sufficient for achieving righteousness. Having listened attentively, Nicodemus knew in his heart that Jesus' words were true. He knew they agreed with the words of the prophets even though these truths had been denied by popular opinion and traditional belief. Nicodemus was now ready to hear the truth, which was about to arrive.

Laodiceans

Are the Laodiceans ready for the next step? Our Lord hopes to have their attention with the pronouncement, "I'm about to vomit you out of my mouth" (Revelation 3:16). It was time to turn their thinking upside down, too. In Revelation 3:17, these people believe that they are rich. Jesus tells them they are poor. They insist that they feel good about themselves while Jesus tells them they are wretched and miserable. They say they are in a good place, with need of nothing, while Jesus tells them they are blind and naked.

The contrast our Lord presents to their self-perception could not be more dramatic. This group needed to acknowledge their problems and come to the light so that the Lord may help them. God wants the Laodiceans to become closer to him, to take up their cross daily, and to follow him.

Were they ready to hear? Were they ready for a change in how they think? The message is an allegory, meant for those to whom it applies. The response will be individual. Each person in "Laodicea" must answer the question. Each of us must decide if we are Laodicean and share their problems. Each of us must decide if Jesus is speaking to us in this passage of warning. All who have listened, if they have ears to hear, are ready for the next step: the revelation of truth.

STEP THREE: *REVEAL TRUTH*

Interlude: Pontius Pilate

To prepare for our discussion of the revelation of truth–to which Jesus' dialogues lead–we will discuss, for a moment, the case of Pilate. Pilate failed to commit to the truth even though, on some level, he glimpsed the truth. Pilate's vacillation stands in contrast to the stance of faith (required of Jesus' disciples) which holds firm in the truth.

The Roman governor, Pilate, held a political position requiring he face many difficult problems every day. As governor of Judea, he had been used to murmurings of insurrection, but this time was different. The high priest and his cohort had brought a man to him accused of stirring up rebellion. Pilate knew this claim was suspect and strange based on the interests of those bringing charges. The leaders of the Jewish nation wanted to be free of the Romans as much as any insurrectionist. Yet, they had brought one of their own kind to be condemned for just this very same alleged crime. Something was amiss.

Pilate must have known of Jesus, his teachings and ministry. Jesus' work had attracted large crowds. Pilate's network of spies was always bringing him information about suspects who were causing excitement among the Jews. It didn't take too much to destabilize the Jews, and the governor had to stay ahead of trouble. Pilate knew enough of this man in front of him to realize that Jesus was no threat to Rome. He inferred that the alleged culprit must have posed a serious threat to the Jewish leadership for otherwise they would not have brought him to trial. Their wish to see him dead made no sense. The Jews always handled this kind of thing themselves by their own laws. Why did Jesus upset the Jewish rulers so?

Pilate could not get much information out of Jesus, who would not even defend himself against the charges. Did this man want to die? He seemed like a man of peace. Even Pilate's wife had had a dream which warned Pilate not to deal with Jesus. Nothing made sense in this situation. Is this man a god as some have claimed? Although Jesus took an interest in Pilate's motives and beliefs, he would not cooperate by divulging further information. He did speak about the truth, though. Pilate thought of truth as an instrument for manipulation and control—or again, as something to be manipulated and controlled. No ultimate truth existed in Pilate's mind.

To Jesus, truth is everything as he declared to Pilate. He came into this world to testify to the truth. He stated to Pilate "Everyone who is of the truth listens to my voice" (John 18:37). Of course, Pilate gave him up to be crucified. Truth for Pilate, at that moment, was pragmatic or opportunistic. Truth involved preventing the riot that would ensue unless Jesus was condemned. How many would he have to kill instead of the one that was the focus of that day's hatred? Although he was not comfortable with his decision, Pilate made what seemed like a reasonable trade-off. Such are the exigencies of business and politics—so Pilate reasoned.

What is truth? Jesus had come to this world to deal in truth. Jesus had prepared the woman at the well, Nicodemus, and the Laodicean church for the truth he needed to share. For that they crucified him, for Jesus himself is the way, the truth, and the life.

The Samaritan Woman

The woman of Samaria was ready to hear the truth that Jesus brought her. He revealed her thoughts and her past and that he was the promised Messiah. He said that God did not wish to be worshipped by the traditions of her people or the rites of the Jews but in "spirit and truth" (John 4:23), free from the rules and institutions of human creation. Stunned, the Samaritan woman had never heard such a truth although she recognized that it was correct. Leaving behind her pitcher, she ran to fetch her townsmen without noticing the disciples who were returning. She was on a mission. She shared her testimony with the men of the village. She became the first missionary (after John the Baptist). "Come, see a man who told me everything that I did. Can this be the Christ?" (John 4:29). Her testimony could not have been more effective.

The men of the village saw the dramatic difference that Jesus' preaching had made in that she had become a new person, herself, the very woman they had known and who now stood, transformed, in front of them. Now, they had to see this man for themselves, the one who had created such a miraculous change. They left immediately for the well. At their invitation, Jesus stayed in their city for two days, sharing the truths of the kingdom of God.

Nicodemus

Overwhelmed by new information, Nicodemus had never expected such a dialogue with the Jewish rabbi nor such an experience. Having transformed his thinking under Jesus' influence, Nicodemus was now ready for truth. What amazing truth he received, truth that changed his life, truth he shared with the world, truth that still reverberates today. Truth still changes lives today, just as it did in the life of Nicodemus.

Jesus revealed to Nicodemus that he was the Son of Man who had descended from heaven. Jesus revealed that he would be crucified for bringing life to those who believe. Like the serpent that Moses lifted up in the wilderness (Numbers 21:8-9), so Jesus would be lifted up, crucified. He revealed that he was on a mission of love and faith (rather than works). He came to save man, not to condemn. He was the light of the world. Whoever could "do the truth" would come to the light.

What a blessing for Nicodemus! Jesus' wonderful message emanated truth, which he recognized in his love for the light. People today who love the light still receive such messages.

The word of God does not reveal many details about the life of Nicodemus after this nocturnal interview. But there is enough evidence to infer that Nicodemus became a believer. Nicodemus later says to the Pharisees, in apparent defense of Jesus:

"Does our law judge a man, unless it first hears from him personally and knows what he does?" (John 7:50-51)

Nicodemus there suggests in front of the Pharisees that Jesus is being treated unfairly. This statement was likely enough to have him excluded from any future plots to destroy Jesus.

The third reference to Nicodemus occurs in John 19:39. He actively helps Joseph of Arimathea to retrieve and bury the body of our Lord after his death. What wonderful truths Nicodemus received, treasured, and shared!

Laodiceans

The Laodiceans are the last to receive the truth, among our three examples. Jesus prepared them to receive the truth. In order to "hear" truth they must be ready to hear, just as the woman at the well and Nicodemus had to become ready.

Unlike the Samaritan woman and Nicodemus, there is no evidence this group received the truth in their hearts. Remember, this passage is an allegory. Those to whom it applies must "hear" his voice and respond. Each person has to self-identify as needing the message. We cannot measure another's response, only our own response. This Laodicean message is directed at each of us.

Jesus clearly gives the solution to the difficult position in which the Laodiceans find themselves. There is a way out, which he longs for them to discover. Revelation 3:18 gives the solution in three parts, symbolically: 1) gold, tried in the fire; 2) white raiment, and 3) eye salve. The solution is clear. Yet, the significance of these symbolic substances, and how to obtain them, remain elusive. The solution, given in Revelation 3:18, contains all the required elements so we may experience the truth. The gold refers to the wealth that comes to us from our sanctification and because of abiding in Jesus Christ. White raiment symbolizes salvation; we are covered by the robe of righteousness. Eye salve indicates the cleansing required so that the believer may experience the fullness of God.

These images will be further discussed in later chapters where we delineate three kinds of relationships that foster our spiritual growth.

Conclusion

The Samaritan woman knew that she had a need and a problem but lacked direction where to find help. Once she met the Savior sent by God at the well, she quickly recognized him as the answer to her heart's desires. Then, she took action on this revelation of truth by preaching to others about Jesus Christ as the Messiah.

Nicodemus felt a need which prodded his heart. He knew exactly where to go. Nicodemus came to Jesus at night and found something he wasn't expecting. He found the true nature of God, which gives new birth. He recognized Jesus as the man whom God had sent. Later, Nicodemus apparently acts upon this truth by defending Jesus to the Pharisees and by honoring him at his burial.

The Laodiceans were not looking for God. These people felt they knew all about God already and needed no further instruction. They stopped listening for God's voice without realizing that they had wandered away from the light. They did not know that they were off the path. Without the light of God's guidance, they cannot find their way back. God can do nothing more for them until they hear his voice. It will be up to each of them to hear and respond to God's special counsel. The Laodiceans had quit looking for God, but God was looking for them.

CHAPTER 3

HOW TO CONNECT TO GOD

The story of the prodigal son is a parable with universal themes, told by Jesus (Luke 15:11-32). The parable describes a predicament all of us share; each of us may take the role of the prodigal son. Like the prodigal son, we have all left home long ago, as children of Adam. Like Adam, we are separated from God. Yet, we may find our way back home just as the prodigal did. The steps that the prodigal son takes in the story delineate the *saving relationship*, which is available to us through the Savior, Jesus Christ. The salvation experience does not involve merely the repentant sinner who takes steps toward the Lord. Our relationship with God is never one-sided. Our Lord has a role to play, both before the believer's action and afterward.

The salvation experience relies upon a *saving relationship*, a relationship between God and each of his people. Neither party alone can make this saving relationship happen. A partnership requires communication, action and response from both parties. Our free will and genuine love can only be preserved through a bilateral relationship.

In this chapter, we will discuss the *saving relationship* and its three steps.

- God reveals himself to us

- We respond to what we have been told
- God completes our salvation

We will illustrate the concept by the biblical story of the prodigal son. Against this backdrop, we will discuss other scriptures which further explain the steps in the *saving relationship* offered through Jesus Christ.

The Prodigal Son

The prodigal was in desperate straits. His money was gone; his friends had left. Food was scarce, as there was a famine in the land and the prodigal was desperately hungry. Reduced to hard labor at a local farm, the prodigal son slept outside. As he fed the hogs one day, he even envied their food. How had he landed in this sorry predicament? How would he get out of this mess?

At one time, his fortunes had seemed to be good and right. When he had left home to start out life on his own, everything was perfect. He knew exactly what to do. He was equipped with money from an inheritance. He had picked out a nice location to make his home, where life would be easy. And things *were* easy until circumstances changed.

The famine seemed to match the despondency which was building in his heart. This new life had not brought the satisfaction for which he had hoped. He had believed he might have a fulfilled life away from his father, in fact, the contrary had been so. Everything became unstable; he could not find love and acceptance in his new life, as much as he desired those good things.

The prodigal, after some time, finally realized the darkness in his life. There was no real love for him here. That which he had believed to be love turned out to be shallow and could not compare to the love from his father, which was deep and constant. His father knew all of his faults and loved him no matter what. The son wanted to go back to his father's house, where true love abounded. This love would not stop when life got hard or when he made mistakes. The prodigal wondered if he could really go back and begin again. There must be a better way! How could he change direction?

During his morning chores that day, he thought of the servants in his father's house. His father had accepted, loved, and taken care of them. Was my father right after all? He considered this question. Then, a change came over him.

He came to himself (Luke 15:17).

An insight crystallized in his mind at just that moment. He could return to his father's house. Suddenly, he became convinced that the path he had chosen had been wrong. His father's way was better. The son longed for what his father had to offer. He immediately knew what he had to do next.

1. I will get up and go to my father, and will tell him, "Father, I have sinned against heaven, and in your sight.
2. I am no more worthy to be called your son. Make me as one of your hired servants."
3. He arose, and came to his father (Luke 15:18-20).

After he "came to himself," the hunger pangs died down. Instead, the prodigal son hungered to be with his father. He realized the emptiness of his existence and that his father's love and acceptance was what he wanted. Thus, the prodigal confessed his wrongs. He repented. And finally, he came back to the father. His father knew he was coming and could not wait for his son to arrive. The father ran to his son. He hugged and kissed him while covering him with a robe, like a wealthy man! Having returned to his father, the prodigal became an esteemed member of his family again, a child of the promise.

This *saving relationship* has steps and designated parts. Our Lord initiates; after that, he stops and waits for us, for he can go no further. Each one of us must respond in our turn, very much like the prodigal. After our response, it is the Lord's turn again, at which point he completes the process with the third step.

First, God reveals.

"How many hired servants of my father's have bread enough to spare, and I'm dying with hunger!" (Luke 15:17).

Second, the prodigal responds:

I will get up and go to my father, and will tell him, "Father, I have sinned against heaven, and in your sight. I am no more worthy to be called your son. Make me as one of your hired servants." ... He arose, and came to his father (Luke 15:18-20).

Third, God completes salvation:

But while he was still far off, his father saw him, and was moved with compassion, and ran, and fell on his neck, and kissed him... But the father said to his servants, "Bring out the best robe, and put it on him. Put a ring on his hand, and shoes on his feet" (Luke 15:20-22).

Such was the prodigal's experience in the New Testament story.

Abraham

Abraham had a similar experience in Genesis of the *saving relationship*.

First, God reveals:

Then Yahweh brought him outside, and said, "Look now towards the sky, and count the stars, if you are able to count them." He said to Abram, "So your offspring will be" (Genesis 15:5).

Second, Abraham responds:

He believed in Yahweh (Genesis 15:6).

Third, God completes salvation:

...who credited it to him for righteousness (Genesis 15:6).

We can see these three steps of the saving relationship throughout the Bible.

The Gospel of John

John 3:16 has these same three steps.
First, God reveals:

For God so loved the world, that he gave his only begotten Son (John 3:16a, KJV).

Second, the believer responds:

That whosoever believeth in him... (John 3:16b, KJV)

Third, God completes salvation:

...shall not perish but have everlasting life (John 3:16c, KJV).

The Book of Revelation

These three steps are about life itself. They are especially demonstrated in Revelation 3:18, 20. Revelation 3:18 is mysterious, containing the counsel of Jesus to the Laodiceans. He gave such counsel to this group to guide them into a true experience with God. The verse tells them they need to do three things to get past the lethargy of their current disconnection from God.

First, they must purchase white raiment, as a garment to wear for a covering, properly to conceal their shame. This white raiment represents the experience of salvation. Their "shame" is their desire to move away from God and live by their own rules. The first thing we need in order to walk and connect with God is a white garment. Thus, our sins are forgiven and covered, just as the prodigal is covered when he receives the robe from his father.

While verse eighteen (v.18) tells us that we need the salvation experience, it does not explain how salvation is to be accomplished. The key that unlocks the white raiment mystery occurs two verses later. Verse twenty (v.20) gives the three-step solution to salvation. This verse demonstrates how to "buy" white raiment. These steps are the same three that are on display in the other parts of the Bible that we have reviewed.

First, God reveals:

Behold, I stand at the door and knock (Revelation 3:20a).

Second, the believer responds:

If anyone hears my voice and opens the door (Revelation 3:20b).

Third, God completes salvation:

Then I will come in to him (Revelation 3:20c).

These three steps exhibit a relationship of the believer with our Lord. No true relationship takes place without communication. No matter the quality of the relationship—good, bad, simple, complex, healthy, or unhealthy—a relationship must have two-way communication. Good friends complain to us for not keeping in touch. They want to hear our voice and to learn what's going on in our lives. They want to share. Our Lord also wants to communicate with us and for us to respond.

These three steps of salvation make up a relationship with God, a *saving relationship*, which is the first of three relationships in the Christian experience.

STEP ONE: *BEHOLD I STAND AT THE DOOR AND KNOCK*

In the most powerful ways, God reveals himself to every person every day. How can people know who he is unless he shows them? When Jesus asked the disciples whom they personally thought he was, Peter confessed what was in his heart,

> "You are the Christ, the Son of the living God." Jesus answered him, "Blessed are you, Simon Bar Jonah, for flesh and blood has not revealed this to you, but my Father who is in heaven" (Matthew 16:16-17).

Peter knew his confession to be true because God had revealed it to him personally. Peter didn't even know *how* he knew. Since Jesus is the Son of God, Jesus is privy to the thoughts and mind of God. So, Jesus revealed to Peter the source of Peter's knowledge and recognition. This blessing of Jesus goes out not just to Peter but also to each person who recognizes the deity of Christ, his special identity and relationship to God. A revelation from God has supernatural origins. God desires that all people may hear His revelations and respond.

God is love. This understanding must be at the foundation of everything we believe about God. Jesus came not to condemn but to save the world (John 3:17). He wants us to love him because we choose to love of our own free will. Our love is always a choice.

We love him because he first loved us (1 John 4:19).

To get us to choose him, God woos us as certainly as a bridegroom woos his intended love. He shows us who he is, expresses his love for us, and draws us to him. To prepare us for receiving His love, God put the model and capacity for love right inside of our hearts and in our human experience. Ideally, the earliest love we experience is in the context of the family. As we mature, we learn more about love from our early friendships. Then, as adults, our love strengthens; love gets deeper and more resilient.

Where do we learn about such love? We ask questions, listen, and watch all around us to determine more about this beautiful mystery. We watch our parents, other adults, our friends. We read books and poetry; we watch movies. Some efforts are better than others, but none are exact or sufficiently powerful. Our research into this vast topic of love leaves us desiring more. We have only found the effects of love, not the mystery of love.

Each of us must experience love before we can know it.

The creation story in Genesis, especially Genesis 2:24, deals with the origins of marriage, based in love.

Therefore, a man will leave his father and his mother, and will join with his wife, and they will be one flesh (Genesis 2:24).

Here is a relationship built on mutual love between two people. The Creator wants such love between husband and wife. A similar relationship binds Jesus as the bridegroom with each of us. To achieve this connection, He draws us in with revelations of God.

No one can come to me unless the Father who sent me draws him, and I will raise him up in the last day (John 6:44).

This statement does not have to mean that God draws only certain people and not others. Rather, the statement suggests that being drawn—and recognizing and responding to that experience—is the only way to connect to Christ. No one can come to God by way of an intellectual decision nor may we do so just because the choice may be popular in our social circle or required by custom. Our motivations need to be genuine and heartfelt. If we think our lives may become better as a result or we are driven by pressures from family, friends, or pastors, then we miss the free and individual decision required for this holy and joyful relationship and for the commitments entailed.

The father in the parable does not initially go after the prodigal. The son knows the way home. The father must wait. However, the relationship is always on the father's terms, even if the initiative seems to come from the son. The son freely returns home. Yet, it is the father who draws him; and when the prodigal repents, God's love (the father's love) is palpable. Similarly, we hear the father through the voice of Jesus (the Son), and we respond. We must freely respond to the invitation. This holy love, between ourselves and God, is a mystery and an experience.

> *"The gatekeeper opens the gate for him, and the sheep listen to his voice. He calls his own sheep by name, and leads them out" (John 10:3).*

What God Reveals

In this first step of the *saving relationship*, our Lord reveals enough about himself so that every person may not only fall in love with him but also make a well-informed decision about who He is. Quite a bit of detail is provided.

1. God is (Hebrews 11:6)
2. He is the one who rewards those that seek him (Hebrews 11:6)
3. He is Creator of the heavens and the earth (Hebrews 11:3)
4. He rewards those who seek righteousness (Matthew 5:6)
5. He reveals the darkness in our lives and shows us how to come to the light (John 16:8)
6. He tells us he loves us more than we can imagine and wants us with him for eternity (John 17:26)
7. He shows us all of his goodness (Exodus 34:6-7)
8. He reveals that if anyone is in Christ, he is a new creation (2 Corinthians 5:17)
9. He tells us he wants to clothe us with the garments of salvation and cover us with the robe of righteousness (Isaiah

61:10)

God's character is made real. His desires are clear. He is waiting for us to respond of our own free will so we may be his bride. He desires us to be joined to him and to become one flesh with him.

How God Reveals

As we have discussed, God reveals himself to all people. We have also discussed what God reveals. The question remaining, in the first step of the *saving relationship*, is the matter of how he reveals himself to all people. The people who met Jesus, listened to him, and even followed him, during his ministry, had a special blessing. They saw Jesus in the flesh, heard his voice, and felt his touch. It was a special time for those who met Jesus during his lifetime. Those who lived before his ministry also enjoyed his presence, for Jesus was no ordinary man. As the Son of God and the Christ, his presence partakes of the qualities of God, transcendent and beyond time. Thus, Elijah had a heartfelt experience with our Lord well before Jesus' ministry on earth. Elijah communicated well with the Christ, his Lord.

After participating in a dramatic display of God's presence and power on Mount Carmel, Elijah became afraid. Jezebel had threatened his life, and he fled to hide from her wrath. God found him and led him to a safe place. God told Elijah to stand on the mountain nearby as He passed by him and spoke to him. This revelation of God to Elijah is the same God, preached and incarnate through Jesus Christ in the New Testament.

> *A great and strong wind rent the mountains, and brake in pieces the rocks before the Lord; but the Lord was not in the wind: and after*

the wind an earthquake; but the Lord was not in the earthquake: And after the earthquake a fire; but the Lord was not in the fire: and after the fire a still small voice (1 Kings 19:11-12).

God spoke to Elijah in a still, small voice. Similarly, God through Jesus Christ speaks to us today, in the same manner, gently and softly. The apostle Paul reveals:

My power is made perfect in weakness (2 Corinthians 12:9).

God doesn't want people to join him out of fear of His power. He wants people to come to Him because of His love and care. In listening for his still, small voice, we must pay attention and be ready. He reveals himself.

Turn your ear, and come to me. Hear, and your soul will live: and I will make an everlasting covenant with you (Isaiah 55:3).

On many occasions Jesus echoes God, intimating his special kinship with the divine. Jesus was heard to say: "He that has ears let him hear." Just as Jesus is the messenger of God, so it is the job of the Holy Spirit to communicate with us so we may know God.

However, when he, the Spirit of truth, has come, he will guide you into all truth, for he will not speak from himself; but whatever he hears, he will speak (John 16:13).

Many examples demonstrate the New Testament revelation. Our Lord has a proven track record of getting people's attention and getting his message presented. The story of Lydia is one example. On Paul's first visit to Asia Minor, he started work in the city of Philippi. He met a woman named Lydia who had moved from Thyatira to the city of Philippi.

> *A certain woman named Lydia, a seller of purple, of the city of Thyatira, one who worshiped God, heard us; whose heart the Lord opened to listen to the things which were spoken by Paul (Acts 16:14).*

This woman worshiped God and heard the Spirit speak to her heart while Paul revealed the word and gospel of Jesus Christ. Choosing to believe God's word, after her baptism, she prevailed upon Paul and Timothy to stay in her house as long as they were in the area.

Another example where Jesus makes a message about God known to his people occurs on the day of his resurrection. This experience happened with two of his disciples who knew him well. They are not his apostles. One of them is named Cleopas and the second man is unnamed.

All the disciples of Jesus are in a quandary after his death. Although he had told the group many times he would be crucified, it never became a reality to them. They could not comprehend how the Son of God, who had displayed such power over nature, could allow himself to be executed. They knew he displayed power and majesty. He healed every disease put in front of him. He restored sight and even entire limbs. The disciples had seen him raise the dead. How could Jesus permit himself to be arrested and killed? They were all still expecting him to establish an earthly kingdom.

Jesus still had a lot to teach his flock and took this moment to instruct these two disciples about the mission of Christ as described in the Old Testament. These two would share this message with the others when the time was right. The two men had left the rest of the disciples in Jerusalem and journeyed home to the town of Emmaus, where they lived. The walk from Emmaus to Jerusalem was a journey of about fifteen miles and would take six to eight hours.

The two men on the road to Emmaus had been in the room with the apostles after the crucifixion and were still with them Sunday morning, the day of the resurrection. Although they had heard the testimony of the women concerning the empty grave, the men were as confused as the apostles. No one knew what was happening. It didn't seem real.

After the two men from Emmaus had left the disciples in Jerusalem and began their walk home, the resurrected Jesus joined them. Incognito and disguised as a stranger while engaging them in conversation, Jesus explained the recent events of the Savior's death while offering passages from the Old Testament to prove that the death of the Redeemer had been required and predicted. When he broke bread with them that evening at one or their houses in Emmaus, "their eyes were opened and they knew him" (Luke 24:31). Later that same evening, Jesus returned to Jerusalem and revealed himself to the apostles and "opened their understanding" (Luke 24:45).

Through the still small voice to Elijah or the mighty preaching of Paul, in the house of Lydia or on the road to Emmaus, by the Holy Spirit or through scriptural proof, God reveals himself. Through Jesus, God's anointed messenger, this revelation continues. Jesus still opens eyes and understanding today, if we hear his knock and open the door.

Another example of revelation concerns the Holy Spirit. The

ways of God are revealed on the day of Pentecost. After Jesus was resurrected, he met with the apostles for forty days. On the day when he was to return to his Father, he told them to wait in Jerusalem after he left until they were baptized with the Holy Spirit.

> *One day when he was eating with them, he told them not to leave Jerusalem. He said, `Wait here for what the Father promised you. I have told you about that promise already. John baptised with water. But you will be baptised with the Holy Spirit when a few days have passed (Acts 1:4-5).*

The Holy Spirit filled them with power ten days later. On the day of Pentecost, Peter preached in Jerusalem with the power of the Holy Spirit. God used Peter in this situation to reveal himself to the people of Jerusalem. As Peter continued to speak, the Holy Spirit convicted the hearts of the listeners.

> *Now when they heard this, they were cut to the heart, and said to Peter and the rest of the apostles, "Brothers, what shall we do?" (Acts 2:37)*

They were cut to the heart because the Spirit revealed their great need of being restored to God.

> *Draw near to God, and he will draw near to you (James 4:8).*

STEP TWO: *IF ANYONE HEARS MY VOICE AND OPENS THE DOOR*

The first part of the *saving relationship* has now been completed. God has revealed himself to us through Christ. Here, the Lord stops and the second part of the relationship begins. Jesus Christ stands in for God so we can respond to God through Jesus, who incarnates the divine fully. Jesus Christ cannot go past the first part, his part, for he has done all he can. He must now wait for us to respond of our own free will to his invitation. What will people do with this revelation? Some have heard God's voice through Jesus, but they have learned quickly to tune it out and to ignore it. Some hear and dismiss God's voice as foolishness for weak people. Some like the voice and the message but don't feel a need to connect with him. And finally, there are those who, like the prodigal and the Samaritan woman at the well, want to be joined with God. Jesus is the true light which enlightens every man. Having seen this light, such believers are drawn to it. People will either come to the light or move away from the light. There is no middle ground. Coming to the light is the path of the prodigal, Abraham, and many others.

> *Yet, looking to the promise of God, he [Abraham] didn't waver through unbelief, but grew strong through faith, giving glory to God, being fully assured that what God had promised he was able also to perform (Romans 4:20-21).*

The prodigal (1) confessed his sins; (2) repented, and (3) came to the father. This decision to come to God cannot be merely an intellectual one. The decision to join with God must come from the heart. Jesus engages the intellect by entering into dialogue with his would-be disciples. Yet, the heart decides to receive the Holy Spirit. When one comes to God is best described as a response to his invitation. Upon receiving the invitation, we have an opportunity for a faith decision. By an act of faith, we accept the invitation. In turn, the Lord will stand by his word and make us one of his people.

This moment of decision by faith is vividly dramatized in the story when Jesus approaches the boat in which the disciples are fighting their way through a terrible storm on the Sea of Galilee (Matthew 14:22-33). They had left Jesus on the shore hours before, at his request, and now find themselves amidst darkness, high waves, and strong winds. As Jesus walks on the water and approaches their boat, the disciples are stunned. Peter, outspoken as always, asks Jesus if he may walk to him on water. Jesus invites Peter to do so. Peter *gets out of the boat* (Matthew 14:29). Peter does not preoccupy himself with the reality of the wind, water, and waves. He *gets out of the boat*. He does not stop to think about the dangers, the possible regrets, or the results. He *gets out of the boat*. His Lord invites him to come, and he responds. The Lord says to come. Peter comes. He gets up and walks towards his Master across the stormy sea. The Lord speaks to each of us with such an invitation. When he calls us to come, it is our is our turn to respond by *getting out of the boat*.

> *In speaking of faith, we must link it to obedience; it is by faithful obedience that we participate in the life of Jesus. Faith obeys or it is no faith at all. We are not called so much to be like Jesus, imitating him, as we are to obey him–Gordon T. Smith.*[2]

This decision to respond to God's call ought not to be motivated by a need to escape punishment nor by the need for the gift of eternal life. Although these things are promised and assured, the decision to connect to Jesus is about our being right with God. We must know and acknowledge that our way has been the way of error. Our choices, our decisions, and our logic have left us empty. We have to recognize that God's way is how we should now live—and not only how we "ought" but how we *want* to live. We desire most in our hearts to let go of the darkness, which we dislike, and to move toward the light. Like the prodigal, we decide to return. Like Abraham, we answer when God calls.

This prayer of salvation can announce our decision to come to Jesus to connect with him.

> *Lord, you have shown me your love. I see what you have done at the cross, and I believe you have done it for me. I confess my sins. I don't want to live in the world of darkness any longer. I cannot fix myself. I come to you now. I give myself to you. I want to be connected to you. I want to be part of you. Amen.*

Once we answer the call and return at God's invitation, we may expect that there will be a cost for our decision. No money is involved. But look what we are buying. Isaiah describes the purchase.

> *Hey! Come, everyone who thirsts, to the waters! Come, he who has no money, buy, and eat! Yes, come, buy wine and milk without money and without price (Isaiah 55:1).*

We are buying the pearl of great price.

> *Again, the Kingdom of Heaven is like a man who is a merchant seeking fine pearls, who having found one pearl of great price, he went and sold all that he had, and bought it (Matthew 13:45-46).*

How much did it cost for this pearl of great price to be provided for us to purchase? The seller always has a cost associated with the item he is selling. This pearl is the kingdom that Jesus preached. Since Jesus embodies God and Jesus is the provider of the pearl, we may say that Jesus himself is the pearl. It cost Jesus everything he had—and everything he was made of—to provide this pearl. The price for us is the same: everything we have and everything we are. What a bargain! The buyer will never be the same.

> *Therefore, if anyone is in Christ, he is a new creation. The old things have passed away. Behold, all things have become new (2 Corinthians 5:17).*

STEP THREE: *I WILL COME TO HIM*

The door has been opened, and it is now the Lord's turn to complete this *saving relationship*. Anxious, the Lord arrives immediately. Remember how the father ran to the prodigal? The Lord is running to all who come to him.

As toward the prodigal, God hugs and kisses us. He puts his robe on us. We are now part of the family, the children of God, children of the promise. We have joined the long line of those who have gone before: Abraham, Moses, Samuel, David, Mary, the apostles, and our many acquaintances who have revealed the love of God. It is now our turn to share our newfound light with others.

> *You are the light of the world...Let your light shine before men; that they may see your good works, and glorify your Father who is in heaven (Matthew 5:14-16).*

Baptism, a public expression of faith, is a sign of the new life we have received and a public statement that we have died to self. Having been buried, we are raised to walk in the newness of life.

Does God have more plans for us? Oh, yes. The best is yet to come. This new connection to him, through the *saving relationship*, is the marriage ceremony, when we begin a new life. We will grow together as one flesh. Our spiritual marriage binds us to the bridegroom from above, Jesus Christ. We will grow together with Jesus Christ in the process of our sanctification.

CHAPTER 4

WHAT IT'S LIKE TO GET CLOSER TO GOD

Sanctification

Salvation is not the *saving relationship* itself but the result of the *saving relationship*. Salvation is represented by the wedding ceremony, when the bride and the bridegroom become connected to one another. This event is an analogy used by Jesus himself. After this initial connection at the wedding, the bride and bridegroom will spend their lifetime together becoming one flesh. Their coming together as one is another analogy that Jesus used for becoming one with him. It is sanctification.

Weddings are perhaps among the most exciting events in life. Two people are drawn together. Privately, they pledge their love and commitment. They decide to be joined legally as a couple. After much planning and preparation, the two come together, usually in front of many witnesses, to make public and powerful vows of love and commitment, similar to the following:

> *I take you to be my wife/husband, forsaking all others, to have and to hold, from this day forward, for better or for worse, for richer, for poorer, in sickness and in health, to love and to cherish, as long as we both shall live.*

The seriousness of this life-changing vow and commitment corresponds to the power of their love. A wedding binds people of different ages and life-positions in a universal celebration. The younger people at a wedding are excited about the event because of the festive atmosphere and the food. The older people are excited for different reasons. Most are still amazed at the hope and promise of new love. Like a new baby, the marriage is fresh. All things are possible. If you are married, you might remember your beginning as a couple and all the excitement, hope, and promise of the moment.

Our Lord created people to give, receive, and share love. We follow this plan for love that is programmed inside of us. A man and a woman separate from family and join to one another to become one flesh. Love gives birth to more love. The wedding starts the process of marriage whereby the two grow together in unity, a process that happens slowly over a lifetime. A couple may face problems which they need to work through together. They set goals. Always communicating, always clinging to each other, always remembering their history together, their relationship becomes sacred, more and more complete. This process does not happen naturally. The effort required does not come from an instinct we are born with. The relationship takes hard work, determination, and self-sacrifice from both individuals. Both partners have to yield self to become one. Such a marriage is the ideal, which is not always realized, although it may be sought.

God's plan of love spans every race, culture, and language. Our feelings are not an accident, for God made us for this love.

Note that the Christian life is defined as knowing or gain-

> ing Christ, and this "knowledge" is not a reference to intellectual understanding but to an experiential encounter with Christ. Paul uses the language of to know the same way it is used to refer to intimacy in marriage – we know Christ intimately – Gordon T. Smith.[3]

The connection that holds couples together provides an analogy for the relationship that God wants with each of us: close, intimate, caring, and full of sharing. The initial connection is salvation whereby we become joined to God in a moment. In our union with him, we change as we walk with God daily. We become closer to God. We become one flesh.

> We all, with unveiled face seeing the glory of the Lord as in a mirror, are transformed into the same image from glory to glory, even as from the Lord, the Spirit (2 Corinthians 3:18).

Daily beholding the Lord, exhibited through Jesus, we become changed into God's image, which is a journey of a lifetime and beyond. Becoming one with God through Jesus is known as *sanctification*. A slow growth over time, sanctification allows us to "come unto the measure of the stature of the fullness of Christ" (Ephesians 4:13). Then we may be "filled with the knowledge of his will in all spiritual wisdom and understanding" (Colossians 1:9). We become holy (1 Peter 1:16), not by our work but by his work of changing our lives.

Imagine a marriage ceremony where the couple leaves each other after the event, and they go their separate ways, living many miles apart. They have no contact. They keep pictures of their spouse, wear their wedding rings, and share the news of their wedding with others. There is no contact and no further communication. None would say this couple had been truly married. They have made no life together nor do they enjoy daily union with each other. The marriage is a sham. Likewise, in our connection with Christ, if there is no union with him after our pledge of love—our commitment, and our baptism—then we have no true connection to Christ.

> *We are united with Christ through God's justifying grace and we grow into union with Christ through God's sanctifying grace – Gordon T. Smith.* [4]

SANCTIFICATION IS BECOMING RIGHTEOUS

As we walk with Jesus daily, He is leading us in the paths of righteousness.

> *Shall we continue in sin, that grace may abound? May it never be! We who died to sin, how could we live in it any longer (Romans 6:1-2).*

> *To be spiritual has only one real purpose. It is a means to an end, not the end itself. The goal of all spiritual exercise must be the goal of righteousness. God calls us to be holy. Christ sets the priority of the Christian life: "But seek first his kingdom and his righteousness, and all these things will be given to you as well" (Matthew 6:33). The goal is righteousness – R.C. Sproul.* [5]

In joining with Jesus Christ, we become righteous as he is righteous. "You shall be holy, for I am holy" (1 Peter 1:16). Righteousness is the goal and our calling from the Lord. Our union with

Jesus is the way toward righteousness. We cannot generate our own righteousness. Good habits, self-control or willpower may change our behavior somewhat, but such efforts will not change our hearts. These methods will not lead us to righteousness.

God wants to give us new habits, which can only be done from the inside out. Our hearts will be changed by our wonderful and mysterious union with Christ. Once we receive a new heart, our habits and behaviors change naturally, instinctively.

Without such a partnership and union, we would be left to go it alone. The power for change and of the Gospel thrive in such partnership. Paul counseled Timothy to avoid contact with those people that adhere to mere forms and formalities of religion while denying its power. This power changes one's life (2 Tim. 3:5).

This dynamic power involves God's ability to come into our lives, with our invitation and cooperation, to remake us in His image. When Adam and Eve disobeyed in the garden, they lost their spiritual connection with God and lost their ability to know the true difference between good and evil. They lost resemblance to His image. They were without God, at least to a painful degree, and on their own.

> *For only love can satisfy love, and love cannot be compelled! To win a person's friendship, you clasp his hand — you do not clench your fist. All genuine affection springs from free volition, and you cannot truly love without the power to choose!–W. Ian Thomas* [6]

Paul had personally united with God through Christ. He relished the union with Christ, which would change him into God's image. The Pauline letters of Ephesians and Colossians call this oneness with Christ the "mystery of the gospel" (Ephesians 6:19) and "Christ in you, the hope of glory" (Colossians 1:27). He praises Christ for his Spirit "which works in me mightily" (Colossians 1:29).

THE POWER OF THE MYSTERY

The power of the mystery is vastly underrated. Few understand the miracle of divine power that can change our lives. Mysteriously, we may feel very little even while we are being profoundly changed.

Jesus spoke of this mystery in the following words to Nicodemus, concerning the Holy Spirit.

> *The wind blows where it wants to, and you hear its sound, but don't know where it comes from and where it is going. So is everyone who is born of the Spirit (John 3:8).*

A theologian comments, similarly and eloquently:

> *Godliness is a mystery! Fail to grasp this fact, and you will never understand the nature of godliness – W. Ian Thomas.*[7]

The "mystery of the gospel" is a strange, wonderful, and powerful force. As powerful as it is, this force remains hidden. We can know some effects of this subtle power without understanding what or how they are happening. By analogy, aging happens so gradually that we don't know it's happening.

Spiritual growth shows the mystery of the Holy Spirit working within us. The Spirit is building the connection between God and us through Christ. Jesus described the kingdom (which is fueled by the power of the Spirit) as being like a plant that grows from seed.

> *"God's Kingdom is as if a man should cast seed on the earth, and should sleep and rise night and day, and the seed should spring up and grow, he doesn't know how" (Mark 4:26-27).*

The creative and mysterious power, which generates life from the seed in this parable, is the same spiritual force that remakes us into His image.

> *How much more is this almighty power needful to advance us to this wonderful new kind of frame, wherein we live and act above all the power of nature, by a higher principle of life than was given to Adam in innocency, even by Christ and His Spirit living and acting in us! – Walter Marshall.* [8]

We cannot completely understand many experiences in life until we experience their opposites. We do not fully know what goodness is until we see evil. We cannot appreciate life in its fullness until we see death. The prodigal did not understand his father's loving care until he experienced a lack of caring in the world. We do not understand the love in our hearts until we experience the results of its removal.

Examining the consequences of death or separation provides evidence of the power of godliness. The act of joining to Christ, or to another person whom we love, can be slow and steady. By contrast, the removal of love through death or separation may be upsetting and even jarring. When a loved one dies, we grieve. We are devastated. When our oneness with another ends, it is as if we are ripped apart. Powerfully, a tremendous ache engulfs our lives. The angst of our loss can debilitate and even lead to death. We adjust over time without ever being the same again, for it is as if we have lost a part of ourselves in losing a loved one. The closer the connection, the more devastating the loss. A similar sense of loss may occur even when we lose a greatly loved pet.

Similarly, divorce can be like grief for many and create a similar void in our hearts. For the children of divorce, their world is torn apart, and they mourn the loss of a relationship between their parents and themselves. A new bond must be created with each parent. The effects of loss never go completely away. The emotional upheaval of a love separation demonstrates the power of the love connection that has evolved. This process of relationship is subtle and slow.

The death of Jesus showed this same kind of separation and loss. As our sacrifice for sin, He took the responsibility for all sins, for all people, for all time. As he bore our sin, the Father had to withdraw out of the life of his "only begotten son." Did Jesus fear the cross? Did he fear the shame, the torture, the pain, the death? Did he want to cling to the life he had here on earth and to extend his earthly efforts? He feared none of these painful realities. He had taught his disciples not to "fear those who kill the body but are unable to kill the soul" (Matthew 10:28). Having come to this earth to become a man, his destiny was the cross. This sacrifice was his passion.

> *Now my soul is troubled. What shall I say? 'Father, save me from this time?' But for this cause I came to this time (John 12:27).*

His "trouble" was neither death nor pain. Instead, Jesus was desperately grieved about separation from his Father. In the Garden of Gethsemane, as he prayed before his arrest and trial, he felt the beginning of this agony of separation. "My soul is very sorrowful, even unto death" (Matthew 26:38). He had become completely one with the Father and longed for a way to rid evil and darkness from this world without having to undergo a terrible separation from the Father. The Father could not change this plan. The plan had been in place before the foundation of the world. However, he could send him comfort. The Father sent an angel to be by his side in the garden "strengthening him" (Luke 22:2-3). All that could be done was done. The agony of Christ continued to increase.

> *Being in agony he prayed more earnestly. His sweat became like great drops of blood falling down on the ground (Luke 22:44).*

The separation grew just as intense as the peace that settled upon him throughout his passion: his arrest, trial, and crucifixion. His torment and pain were renewed on the cross as he suffered the agony of complete separation from the Father.

> *About the ninth hour Jesus cried with a loud voice, saying, "Eli, Eli, lama sabachthani?" That is, "My God, my God, why have you forsaken me?" (Matthew 27:46)*

And finally:

> *Jesus, crying with a loud voice, said, "Father, into your hands I commit my spirit!" Having said this, he breathed his last (Luke 23:46).*

As Jesus cried out these words, God's absence from the Son was complete. The Father's presence had been ripped away from Jesus within just a few hours. At this moment of complete withdrawal and separation from the Father, Jesus died. The power of this mystery on the cross is beyond our comprehension.

THE MODEL OF THE MYSTERY

When Adam and Eve sinned, they became separated from God. The mission of Christ is to reconcile this separation and make it possible for humankind to reconnect with God.

> *We beg you on behalf of Christ, be reconciled to God. He made him who knew no sin to be sin on our behalf, so that we might become the righteousness of God in him (2 Corinthians 5:20-21).*

When Adam and Eve disobeyed in the garden of Eden, they created a giant chasm between themselves and God. Their rift had to be reconciled. This reconciliation of humankind to God is bigger than most people think. God had to resolve the differences between himself and his new creation who had chosen to go their own way. If he could not resolve this conflict, he could not establish the kingdom he had planned, which would last forever without sin. The model of God's relationship to his created beings now had to change, because his people had changed.

Humanity is full of conflict. We see and experience these conflicts daily, as a large part of our lives and a defining feature of our experiences. Conflicts take place concerning money and family. We all have financial limitations. The price of things goes up, and our resources are always lagging. The apparent discrepancy between our needs and our resources causes conflict.

A couple might not agree on their spending decisions as their budget gets stretched. Now, things get personal. More serious conflicts are always personal. Perhaps one spouse thinks the other is not helping enough. The children are not getting along. Perhaps other relatives are criticizing. Conflicts multiply. Feelings are hurt. Problems happen at work, at school, in church, with friends, family, and neighbors. Unexpected illnesses or loss of family income put extra strain on the relationship.

Some conflicts need to be resolved while others we let continue. Often, we may not know how to resolve them. Some conflicts are resolved by time alone. "Time heals all wounds," as the saying goes. Of course, time does not heal all wounds. Some even say that "time wounds all that heals." Staying healed requires intention and effort.

Antagonistic parties can talk out conflicts so they may be resolved. Some require an intermediary or a third party to intercede. This third party is usually a neutral person who is fair and able to understand both sides. This mediator can help resolve the issue, or at least make it better. Even animals in social groups have used a third party for conflict resolution. However, no conflict can be resolved if neither party wants a resolution. If only one party wants the conflict to end, the mediator will fail, and the breach will not be repaired.

There was a conflict in the garden of Eden. Adam and Eve had gone against the express wishes of God. They were told they could eat anything they wanted in the garden except the fruit of the tree of the knowledge of good and evil.

God had told them:

"For in the day that you eat of it, you will surely die" (Genesis 2:17).

The serpent had told Eve just the opposite:

"You won't surely die, for God knows that in the day you eat it, your eyes will be opened, and you will be like God, knowing good and evil" (Genesis 3:4-5).

Both Adam and Eve ate the fruit. This act created conflict between them and God. They had separated from God. Unaware of the exact problem, the couple realized their shame before God. However, they did not understand the significance of their wrong choice. God had warned them that if they ate of this tree, they would die. Since they had never witnessed or experienced death, they did not understand it.

The problem of their separation from God seemed impossible. Adam and Eve couldn't go back and undo their action. Unless God allowed his recent creation to expire, or to suspend the rule mandating death, the two parties would be at an impasse with no clear resolution. God is love. So the destruction of his recent creation was not on the table. Neither could he change his rule lest he be inconsistent or unjust. This vital rule had been established to protect the garden of Eden. Without this rule in place, God's reign and his future kingdom (as he had planned it) would be thwarted.

In God's omniscience, God had foreseen the lapse from Eden. He had a resolution that would satisfy both parties. The Son of God became the mediator. Only by the Son could this separation be reconciled. The Son would take a position between the Father and humankind. All communication to and from the Father with humankind would be through the Son. Jesus's life made this role possible. Jesus could remain in the Father. Humankind could be in Jesus. So, through Jesus's mediation, a reunion with the Father became possible. The life and death of Jesus extend righteousness to all those who have heard and responded to his voice. Humankind would be united with God through Jesus. Jesus would be united with humankind and with God. The Father is in the Son, and the Son is in the Father. The Holy Spirit provides the communication that holds these relationships together.

> *But all things are of God, who reconciled us to himself through Jesus Christ (2 Corinthians 5:18).*

> *In that day you will know that I am in my Father, and you in me, and I in you (John 14:20).*

Humanity would no longer be directly in union with the Father and connected with him as Adam had been. They would be connected to the Father through the Son.

> *For there is one God, and one mediator between God and men, the man Christ Jesus (1 Timothy 2:5).*

> *For if, while we were enemies, we were reconciled to God through the death of his Son, much more, being reconciled, we will be saved by his life (Romans 5:10).*

The parable of the vine reinforces this threefold relationship (John 15:1-5). The Father is the vine keeper. He takes care of the garden and provides rich, life-giving soil. Jesus is the vine, which has its roots in the soil. We are the branches, connected to the vine. The vine receives nourishment from the soil. The branches receive nourishment from the vine. The vine stands between the branches and the soil.

JESUS LIVED THE MYSTERY

When Jesus lived on this earth, He lived the model of the mystery. Christ as a man lived as a man. He used none of his divinity. He completely depended on the Father and did nothing on his own. The works he did were the Father's works, by the Father's power through the Son.

> *The Son can do nothing of himself, but what he sees the Father doing. For whatever things he does, these the Son also does likewise (John 5:19).*
>
> *I can of myself do nothing. As I hear, I judge, and my judgment is righteous; because I don't seek my own will, but the will of my Father who sent me (John 5:30).*
>
> *For I spoke not from myself, but the Father who sent me, he gave me a commandment, what I should say, and what I should speak (John 12:49).*
>
> *When you have lifted up the Son of Man, then you will know that I am he, and I do nothing of myself, but as my Father taught me (John 8:28).*

Totally dependent on the Father, Jesus had to deny himself. Instead of relying on his own power, he relied on the power of the Father. Jesus' nature differed greatly from ours. His nature was divinity. He could have acted by this divine nature at any time, but he did not. He gave up this privilege, and denied his divinity, to depend on the Father.

> *Have this in your mind, which was also in Christ Jesus, who, existing in the form of God, didn't consider equality with God a thing to be grasped, but emptied himself, taking the form of a*

servant, being made in the likeness of men. And being found in human form, he humbled himself, becoming obedient to death, yes, the death of the cross (Philippians 2:5-8).

Don't you believe that I am in the Father, and the Father in me? The words that I tell you, I speak not from myself; but the Father who lives in me does his works (John 14:10).

If we want to live for Jesus, we will live as he did by his example. As he submitted to his Father, we will submit to the Father through the Son. Jesus denied self and obeyed his Father. Our work is to deny self and obey the Father through the Son.

If anyone desires to come after me, let him deny himself, take up his cross, and follow me (John 9:23).

THE EXPERIENCE OF THE MYSTERY

Like love, the mystery of godliness is inexpressible. We can read or talk about godliness and love, but the experience of them remains deeply personal. A false mystery gathers steam from willpower and determination. We may like willpower better than surrender because willpower puts us in control of our actions and behavior. Willpower may change our behavior, but willpower will never change our hearts.

You may have found and come to know God in the Lord Jesus Christ, receiving Him sincerely as your Redeemer, yet if you do not enter into the mystery of godliness and allow God to be in you the origin of His own image, you will seek to be godly by submitting yourself to external rules and regulations and by conformity to behavior pat-

terns imposed upon you by the particular Christian society that you have chosen and in which you hope to be found acceptable – W. Ian Thomas. [9]

But now it has been revealed to his saints, to whom God was pleased to make known what are the riches of the glory of this mystery among the Gentiles, which is Christ in you, the hope of glory; whom we proclaim, admonishing every man and teaching every man in all wisdom, that we may present every man perfect in Christ Jesus; for which I also labor, striving according to his working, which works in me mightily (Colossians 1:26-29).

The experience of the mystery lies inside of us. Jesus said, "God's kingdom is within you" (Luke 17:21). Stop to consider how the kingdom may work within us, even without our becoming robots or losing our free will. This power of union with Christ within his people is a great mystery.

THREE LEVELS OF HUMAN FUNCTIONING

The unity brought about by Christ, between God and the human being, can be further explained by considering the makeup of ourselves and society according to three levels of functioning. Jesus Christ responds to us according to our unique attributes in this threefold pattern.

Everything we do in this world seems to require three levels of functioning. No matter the end results, all three levels are working together. Whether baking a cake, digging a ditch, or running a country, the same three levels are constantly in action.

The first level encompasses a vision of ideals, goals, and desires, whether the values of the group or the individual are at stake. This first level could be called *the level of values*. At this level, we answer questions about who we are, why we are here, and what goals we have.

The second level relates to decisions. Once values have been established, we make decisions based on these values and other input. We make specific plans and decisions about how to achieve our goals.

The third level pertains to action. At the first two levels, nothing is actually done. Ideas and inputs are received. Decisions are made. Nothing is produced or accomplished. No movement occurs. The action phase is where things get done. We get out of the chair and accomplish. We can write a plan, get dressed, buy materials, create a drawing, or build a bookcase. These actions follow decisions, which unfold after evaluation of our values, standards, and beliefs.

Sensory input may come to our decision maker to report that we are hungry. The decision maker calculates how long it has been since we ate last and the demands of our current schedule. Decisions are calculated based on the kind of food on hand. At the value level, we measure our food choices for their nutritional or energetic effect. One person's action center may direct that he or she eat junk food, while another's may direct the eating of soup, salad, and French bread. A third person may eat a hamburger and fries. The same steps are taken by all three people, but the results are quite different because of each person's different values and desires.

Besides the values level, which differs among people, the decision-making process also varies. Some are more analytical than others. Some are more emotional. Some are more easily influenced by outside input. Many are incredibly independent. We are all amazingly different. God likes it like that way, for he made us to be unique individuals. Our individuality remains even while we are united with the Lord.

It is no coincidence that governments also operate on these three levels. The values level is where the governing constitution resides. The constitution is interpreted and enforced by the judicial system. The dreams and ideals of a country are its guiding light.

The legislative body of a country makes the decisions for the country based on guidance by values and other input. These decisions are put forth in the form of laws and programs that govern the country.

The executive branch is the action center that implements the laws and programs created by the decision makers. These three levels of functionality are at work in every government, business, school, family, and individual. Even a solo business operates according to these three levels. In this case, a single person will set values, make decisions, and do the work (including sweeping the floors).

The values and ideals of a country constitute its heart. Similarly, the heart of a country, a company, or a person resides in its values. These values guide decisions and actions. But even people with similar or the same values will have different results. Any single value may be filtered through each person's unique decision-making function; in each instance, different results will happen. The results may be compatible. However, we are not robots, built to conform and do exactly the same things as others. We are all unique, endowed with different minds and skills, even when we share certain values.

Jesus called the value center the "heart." The Old Testament and Psalms also called it by this name. Paul referred to the same as "our spirit." This center, the heart or the spirit, is where the Holy Spirit will reside.

> *But he who is joined to the Lord is one spirit (1 Corinthians 6:17).*

> *That Christ may dwell in your hearts through faith (Ephesians 3:17).*

THE NEW HEART EXPERIENCE

Adam and Eve lost this heart center when they did things their way and to disobey God. We need to accept and encourage such a connection from the heart when we seek God's presence in our lives. At the values level of the heart, our spirit is bound to Christ's spirit. Once we have this bond, we can return to the image of God. If we do not have this connection, we are left to go through life alone. Our only guide will be our self-oriented will. We will only consider what is important for ourselves without God's direction or a divinely sanctioned value system. We must have the spiritual connection, at the heart level, to be the person who God has intended us to be.

> *With the loss of the God-like nature God had given him, man had forfeited the destiny of his being, which was to be like God. In short, man had ceased to be man–Dietrich Bonhoeffer.* [10]

Salvation does not amount to a pragmatic deal or self-interested contract with God. There is no *quid pro quo* between God and his people. We do not make pledges of allegiance to him in exchange for his agreement to save us. We can only deny self and come to him in faith at God's call and request.

Sanctification is not a calculated strategy, either, whereby we decide the correct Christian behavior to perform. Like salvation, sanctification comes by faith. We are restored to the divine values which are placed within our hearts. Correct behaviors then instinctively happen without our being aware of the process—so long as the self does not interfere. The rule of self prevents sanctification. We must participate with God in removing self-direction from our value system. Paul explains this self-sacrifice and dying to self to the Corinthians: "I die daily" (1 Corinthians 15:31).

By falling on the rock so we may be broken (Matthew 21:44), we give up our self-directed life and receive God's values. We enter into the mystery of godliness. If we do not fall upon the rock, then we stumble; we exchange a God-directed life for the self-directed life, and the life of grace for the death of works-righteousness.

In the self-directed life, we try to establish our own rules for Christian living and to measure right and wrong. To stumble is to be governed by the "works of the law." Such works encompass not merely the ten commandments and other requirements accepted by Christians but also manmade rules we manufacture to seem "holy." Such works of the law involve living by the "flesh" (in Christian terminology). When we fall on the rock by giving up self, we live by the Spirit instead of the flesh, just as Jesus taught Nicodemus. Paul wrote about this life in the Spirit in his letter to the Romans.

> *What shall we say then? That the Gentiles, who didn't follow after righteousness, attained to righteousness, even the righteousness which is of faith; but Israel, following after a law of righteousness, didn't arrive at the law of righteousness. Why? Because they didn't seek it by faith, but as it were by works of the law. They stumbled over the stumbling stone. (Romans 9:30-32).*

At the values level, God "puts his law into our heart and writes it in our mind" (Heb. 10:16). The law is there "fulfilled in us" by God (Rom. 8:4). As he corrects our values, we are being restored in his image. Our new values, affecting the decision level of our being, will guide our choices and our action automatically. Our individuality and autonomy continue to be honored.

James writes that sin starts with the "lusts (or desires) that are in our own heart" (James 1:14-15). When we cooperate with God in renewing our spirit, these evil desires will be slowly eliminated; our values change, our lives transform, and we will bear fruit. A powerful force works within us to mend and uplift our hearts. Paul describes this spiritual power as "working in him mightily" (Colossians 1:29). The Old Testament refers to this spiritual transformation as circumcision of the heart.

> *Yahweh your God will circumcise your heart, and the heart of your offspring, to love Yahweh your God with all your heart, and with all your soul, that you may live (Deuteronomy 30:6).*

The psalmist longs for this new heart:

> *Create in me a clean heart, O God. Renew a right spirit within me (Psalm 51:10).*

Jesus speaks of a clean and new heart in the Sermon on the

Mount when he blesses the "pure in heart" (Matthew 5:8). Jesus also proclaims: "For out of the heart come forth evil thoughts" (Matthew 15:19). While he walked with his followers on earth, he corrected them for their hard or even their slow hearts. His followers should love God totally, "with all their heart" (Luke 10:27). This type of love for God is not possible in our natural state, wherein we are unconnected to God. Only when we are connected to God's Spirit and our hearts and spirits have been renewed can we truly love in a holy way befitting of God. In our state without sanctification, we do not even know what love is. This heart transformation is not rapid; certainly, it does not happen as fast as we would like. God knows what is best, however, and it will be done on the divine schedule.

> *I will also give you a new heart, and I will put a new spirit within you; and I will take away the stony heart out of your flesh, and I will give you a heart of flesh (Ezekiel 36:26).*

Our job throughout this process of sanctification is to stay connected and to abide in Christ. His job is to change our hearts. This new heart experience is something to look forward to and enjoy. The same power that draws us to Christ and invites us to come to him is the power that causes us to deny self and to follow as his disciples. We are convicted of our unrighteousness and know that he is the righteousness for all. Like Abraham, we are looking to the promises of God.

> *Yet, looking to the promise of God, he [Abraham] didn't waver through unbelief, but grew strong through faith, giving glory to God, and being fully assured that what he had promised, he was also able to perform (Romans 4:20-21).*

Christ gave this promise in a beatitude: "Blessed are those who hunger and thirst after righteousness, for they shall be filled" (Matthew 5:6). He begins to fill or to change our hearts. We will feel differently in this process. Can we tell what is happening? We still have to get up in the morning and do our work for the day. Our problems may not be changed nor do we have instant solutions. We are changing, not the world around us. The change is slow and subtle but real. Paul called this agent for change the "power that works in me mightily" (Colossians 1:29). Paul knew he was being made new, even though he still had an evil disposition inside of him that fought for control.

> *For the good which I desire, I don't do; but the evil which I don't desire, that I practice. But if what I don't desire, that I do, it is no more I that do it, but sin which dwells in me (Romans 7:19-20).*

Even during the experience of heart renewal, we will still have sinful desires. However, there is a good result to this internal conflict.

> *For I don't know what I am doing. For I don't practice what I desire to do; but what I hate, that I do. But if what I don't desire, that I do, I consent to the law that it is good (Romans 7:15-16).*

Our disdain for the sin in our life and for the stray, evil thoughts which may sweep through our minds signifies that we on the right path—although we are not yet fully connected to the Lord (for the process takes time). Paul recognized and hated his sin. The Spirit's work causes us to recognize and hate sin in our lives, too. As we cooperate with God, the Spirit fills our life. We will bear fruit. We may not recognize this spiritual change but people around us will.

The Pauline letter to the Ephesians sums up the fruits of spiritual growth:

> *But the fruit of the Spirit is love, joy, peace, patience, kindness, goodness, faith, gentleness, and self-control (Ephesians 5:22-23).*

WE REMAIN UNAWARE OF OUR SANCTIFICATION OR BEARING OF FRUIT

This fruit comes into being as the branch grows. We remain unaware of the growth of the fruit or of the fruit itself.

> *There are many works of the flesh, but only one fruit of the Spirit. Works are done by human hands, fruit thrusts upward and grows all unbeknown to the tree which bears it. Works are dead, fruit is alive, and bears the seed which will bring forth more fruit. Works can subsist on their own, fruit cannot exist apart from the tree. Fruit is always the miraculous, the created; it is never the result of willing, but always a growth–Dietrich Bonhoeffer.* [11]

The reason we are not aware of our life changes, and our fruit-bearing, is that our new behavior is involuntary. It seems to us as we are just doing our duty. According to our new frame of reference, such behavior is normal. We are not aware of it. Life-saving heroes may articulate such sentiments in interviews with the press. They believe that their heroic actions are just a part of their job. "Anyone would have done this," they tell the curious inquirer. These heroic actions are instinctive to them.

Jesus explained such instinctive goodness in the parable of the servant and the master:

> *Even so you also, when you have done all the things that are commanded you, say, "We are unworthy servants. We have done our duty" (Luke 17:10).*

Similarly, the sheep, in the parable of the sheep and the goats, instinctively do good. When Jesus invites the sheep into the kingdom, they feel unwilling and unworthy. They feel that their worthy deeds amounted to nothing special and merely the execution of their duty (Matthew 25:31-46). Such is the experience of all of Christ's followers.

Besides this instinctive behavior, another reason we may not directly feel the righteousness of sanctification is that our behavior reflects God's efficacy and presence working through us. Our new behavior thus becomes natural to us. We no longer think about what should be done or how we should act. We automatically act as the consequence of the law written on our hearts.

> *For when Gentiles who don't have the law do by nature the things of the law, these, not having the law, are a law to themselves, in that they show the work of the law written in their hearts (Romans 2:14-15).*

Our behaviors and interests will change without our thinking about making such changes. If our behavior is not natural (instinctive), it is not from God. If we base our behavior on what we decide for ourselves or on the expectations of others, we are being guided by "works of the flesh." Instinctive behavior, as the result of spiritual practice, flows from the heart and from God. While willpower can make people believe that we love them (even when we do not), love from our heart is instinctive and without pretense.

On the spiritual level, instinctive behavior springs from God who is working in us. If we believe we are falling short of our Lord's requests, the Holy Spirit will make us aware of such lack. The Spirit has the job of showing us failures and shortcomings while inviting us to acknowledge these issues so they may be put into the Lord's hands for him to resolve.

Our spiritual growth will make our old way of living gradually disappear as we become one with Christ. We will slowly begin to live the God-directed life. We will never know in advance the good things the Lord has in store for us, day by day, as we become available to him. Paul told the Corinthians:

All are yours, and you are Christ's, and Christ is God's (1 Corinthians 3:22- 23).

CHAPTER 5

GETTING CLOSER TO GOD THROUGH WORSHIP

The Abiding Relationship

Sanctification results from a mutual indwelling. Christ abides in the Father, we abide in Christ, and Christ abides in us (John 14:20). As we abide in Christ, we receive sanctification. Thus, like branches of a vine which are fed by a divine source, we are spiritually nourished.

New Christians should be excited to enter into this relationship with the Lord. They should be thrilled. Every new bride is eager for her upcoming wedding. The promise of a new life together, with the person of her dreams, offers endless delights. It is natural to wish to sustain and keep alive forever this joyous feeling. If we compare a new Christian to a bride and Jesus to the bridegroom, how can we keep alive the love that binds and delights us?

Any marriage will suffer if one partner takes the other for granted. There is a way we can help keep this spark of love alive. We can take part in the marriage so that our love never dies. In fact, Jesus gives us the *abiding relationship* as a sure way for sustaining the love between ourselves (who are all metaphorically "brides") and himself (the bridegroom).

The *abiding relationship* is the second of three relationships with God. The first is the *saving relationship*, which we have discussed earlier in Chapter 3. Once we have received salvation, we are to be sanctified, as discussed in Chapter 4.

Sanctification results from the *abiding relationship*. This second relationship provides for our life and our walk with Jesus daily. It completes our union with him over time. The goal of this relationship is for each person to grow and to become one with Christ. As we participate in an abiding love with our Lord, we will be continually filled with his Spirit. Just as we will need to do our part to keep the relationship fresh—honest and authentic—so our new partner will always do his part and never let us down. Jesus Christ is always true to the vows that God has pledged to and for us since Christ embodies God.

> *Can a woman forget her nursing child that she should not have compassion on the son of her womb? Yes, these may forget, yet I will not forget you! Behold, I have engraved you on the palms of my hands (Isaiah 49:15-16).*

Just as Jesus invited us to come to the cross, so we are invited every day to take up our cross and follow him. Jesus still reveals God to us and teaches us to be holy as he is holy. Our branch has been connected to the tree, and we're being fed from the root.

> *You, being a wild olive, were grafted in among them, and became partaker with them of the root and of the richness of the olive tree (Romans 11:17).*

Colossians gives us a general idea of how to proceed after we are connected to the vine.

As therefore you received Christ Jesus, the Lord, walk in him (Colossians 2:6).

We were saved by faith, and we will be sanctified by faith.

Righteous people are known by their fruit. They become holy by the sanctifying power of the Holy Spirit working in them and on them. The Holy Spirit knows what holiness is. He is called the Holy Spirit not only because He is holy Himself but also because He is working to produce holiness in us–R.C. Sproul.[12]

Any works we do by our own strength do not contribute to our sanctification in the eyes of God. Any of God's works are done through us by Christ.

Godliness is not the consequence of your capacity to imitate God but the consequence of His capacity to reproduce Himself in you–W. Ian Thomas. 13

Some things can be done to cooperate with the process of our sanctification. Without our "help"—or, more correctly, our participation—Christ can do nothing for us. He cannot perform works through us without our cooperation since nothing can be done against our will.

To learn about the *abiding relationship*, which will take us through to continue the process of sanctification, we must look to the same scriptures that are pertinent to the *saving relationship*. The counsel of Jesus to the Laodiceans (Revelation 3:18) tells us what we need to be saved. The explanation in a nearby verse (Revelation 3:20) tells us how to get these provisions:

> *I counsel you to buy from me gold refined by fire, that you may become rich; and white garments, that you may clothe yourself, and that the shame of your nakedness may not be revealed; and eye salve to anoint your eyes, that you may see (Revelation 3:18).*

Before we can participate in the *abiding relationship*, we must have received the white garment from our Lord. When salvation is complete, we can then acquire the gold, refined by fire. This gold is the heavenly wealth that Jesus offers for sale, denoting sanctification, which occurs through Christ in you. Sanctification is the outcome of the *abiding relationship* though it starts earlier with the *saving relationship*. The sequence of items is justified, here, since we cannot buy gold unless we are wearing Christ's robe.

This gold is not ore pulled out of the ground. Infinitely more valuable than earthly gold, this spiritual gold is not duly appreciated by the Laodiceans. The problem with the Laodiceans is in their overestimation of the wealth that they believe belongs to them.

> *Because you say, 'I am rich, and have gotten riches, and have need of nothing;' and don't know that you are the wretched one, miserable, poor, blind, and naked (Revelation 3:17).*

Although the Laodiceans have accumulated worldly wealth, they lack the wealth of God. They mistakenly believe their worldly wealth to be an indicator of spiritual wealth. God accuses them of being wretched, miserable, poor, blind, and naked, despite their bank accounts or how they may feel about themselves. The gold that Jesus has for sale would have filled the Laodiceans with spiritual wealth. For those of us who choose to be close to the Lord, our worldly status is not of value in the community of Christ. We can be young or old, newly baptized or long-time followers. We can be rich or poor. We all share the same need, and we are all equally invited to be enriched by the gold of the true wealth that Christ supplies.

Jesus himself speaks of wealth frequently during his earthly ministry. It is common for Jesus to speak of the dangers of hoarding worldly wealth.

> *Don't lay up treasures for yourselves on the earth, where moth and rust consume, and where thieves break through and steal; but lay up for yourselves treasures in heaven, where neither moth nor rust consume, and where thieves don't break through and steal; for where your treasure is, there your heart will be also (Matthew 6:19-21).*

> *No one can serve two masters, for either he will hate the one and love the other; or else he will be devoted to one and despise the other. You can't serve both God and Mammon (Matthew 6:24).*

When our treasure is in heaven, our hearts will be there also. Our hearts always follow our treasure. It is the way we are made. Colossians adds more detail to this principle. Notice how Laodicea is included in these verses of Colossians. Since the two places were only ten miles apart, both cities were certain to hear this letter read aloud; the letter would circulate between them.

> *For I desire to have you know how greatly I struggle for you, and for those at Laodicea, and for as many as have not seen my face in the flesh; that their hearts may be comforted, they being knit together in love, and gaining all riches of the full assurance of understanding, that they may know the mystery of God, both of the Father and of Christ, in whom are all the treasures of wisdom and knowledge hidden (Colossians 2:1-3).*

The mystery of God contains the heavenly treasures, the wisdom and knowledge of God. This treasure must be pursued. This treasure, described as gold refined by fire, will neither rust nor corrode. The wealth of God is equivalent to "Christ in you, hope of glory" (Colossians 1:27). All other types of treasures will fail us. His treasure will be forever. This treasure represents sanctification.

Parable of the Talents

Jesus tells a complex parable about spiritual wealth, found in Matt. 25:14-30 and Luke 19:11-27. The parable describes the process of sanctification.

A nobleman goes away from his estate. He gives each of his servants an amount of gold and instructs them to do business with this amount until he returns. One of the servants does nothing with the gold. Instead, he hides the wealth while his master is away. When the nobleman returns, this servant has nothing to show beyond the original gold. The other servants follow their master's advice and do business with their gold. When the nobleman returns, they each show him the increase on the original gold they have first received.

The nobleman is Jesus, who has gone away and is waiting to return. His followers are the servants. The first gold that we receive, as the servants do, comes from our connection with Christ during our salvation experience. This gold is the first step in our growth and in the process of the "two becoming one." Similar to earnest money, with which people may start a business, this initial investment is the money with which one can make more money. In 2 Corinthians, Paul describes this initial investment as a down payment of the spirit after believers have received the robe of righteousness.

> *Now he who made us for this very thing is God, who also gave to us the down payment of the Spirit (2 Corinthians 5:5).*

This down payment is the starter gold we receive for buying more gold. The *abiding relationship* allows us to invest continually in the wealth of God by buying gold that has been tried in fire. Through the symbolism of these purchases, we are becoming one with God through Christ as our union with Christ grows closer.

The portion of Rev. 3:18 that speaks of buying gold pertains to sanctification through the *abiding relationship*. However, it is in the second part of Rev. 3:20 that this method for sanctification is further described. This verse describes both the process of salvation and that of sanctification.

Salvation

> *Behold, I stand at the door and knock. If anyone hears my voice and opens the door, then I will come in to him…*

Sanctification

> *…and will dine with him, and he with me (Revelation 3:20).*

After salvation, there will be a dining event with Jesus, which represents the sanctification experience. What can be made of this? The arrangement of these few words suggests a two-way relationship or an *abiding relationship*. As we have discussed above, sanctification may be compared to investment in gold. The dining experience is another metaphor for the *abiding relationship*.

DINING TOGETHER WITH JESUS

Blessed are those who are invited to the marriage supper of the Lamb (Revelation 19:9).

Food has been connected with righteousness ever since Eden. The tree of the knowledge of good and evil, with its fruit, existed in the garden of Eden even before the creation of Adam and Eve. According to Genesis 1, trees were created on the fifth day of creation, and God's first two people were made on the sixth day. They were instructed that they could eat of all the trees of the garden except this one tree. The consequences of violating this prohibition were also clear.

You may freely eat of every tree of the garden; but you shall not eat of the tree of the knowledge of good and evil; for in the day that you eat of it, you will surely die (Genesis 2:16-17).

The plan had been set in place. Eating the fruit would result in death. Since they both ate of the fruit, they were condemned to die. Once Jesus came to earth, he re-confirmed the association between food and righteousness in the Sermon on the Mount:

Blessed are those who hunger and thirst after righteousness, for they shall be filled (Matthew 5:6).

The desire for the righteousness of God, according to this beatitude, will feel like hunger pangs. However, these desires may be satisfied and filled. Thus, he blessed those that had this hunger. These blessed ones are his people, even today.

This theme regarding food and righteousness is continued in the story of the city of Capernaum, described in John 6:1-58. Having been fed by a miraculous multiplication of loaves and fish the day before, the multitudes had been looking for Jesus, who had already reached the city. When they tried the day before to make him king, Jesus seemed to disappear. Jesus knew that such followers were only interested in the food that nourishes the body and had no interest in spiritual rewards. He directs them to seek the food which "remains to eternal life" (John 6:27). As the conversation continues, Jesus reveals that his message requires personal righteousness. Eternal life may be gained by eating his flesh and drinking his blood. This association between food (i.e., his own flesh and blood) and eternal life astonishes his listeners, many of whom were offended by his teaching and departed, never to return.

This is the bread which comes down out of heaven, that anyone may eat of it and not die (John 6:50).

In the Garden of Eden and in the ministry of Christ, eating the forbidden fruit in the garden results in death while eating the bread sent from heaven results in eternal life. To eat the bread of Christ is to participate in the New Covenant. The psalmist recommends that we "taste and see that the Lord is good" (Psalm 34:8 NASB). Jeremiah proclaims, "Your words were found, and I ate them; and your words were to me a joy and the rejoicing of my heart" (Jeremiah 15:16). These scriptures show the depth of the divine presence, which can be ingested through the bread and body of Christ.

Word and sacrament are not ends in themselves. They

are a means by which we meet Christ in real time. The Lord's Supper, for example, is not merely a remembrance of Christ and his work but an actual dynamic and real-time participation in the life of Christ–Gordon T. Smith.[14]

When we hunger and thirst after righteousness, we come to the "supper table of the Lamb" (Revelation 9:9). We are already invited. Jesus is waiting for us. This table is the only place where our hunger can be satisfied.

The parable of the wedding feast (Matthew 22:1-14) establishes the guidelines for our eating with Jesus Christ. The king, who holds a wedding feast for his son, invites many guests. However, many of those invited refuse to come. He keeps inviting more and more people until the banquet hall is full. All who come to the banquet are wearing wedding garments, which the king provided. However, one man makes it to the table without a wedding garment. When the king recognizes his lack of a robe, this unclad man is removed from the banquet hall.

The garments that each guest wears, together with an invitation by the king, identifies him or her as belonging to God's people. Each guest will have experienced the three steps of salvation, leading to the marriage feast. Those who do not accept the invitation for salvation and the robe of righteousness (provided by salvation) cannot dine with Jesus at the table to participate in the *abiding relationship*. Anyone without a robe will not care to eat the flesh or drink the blood of Christ. The pursuit of righteousness, through dining and the *abiding relationship*, is of no concern to those who have not been first joined to Christ.

A similar experience concerning the robe of righteousness is shared in the story of the prodigal. The prodigal is invited to come to the father's house. He responds and accepts the invitation. He is welcomed by his father, who covers him with a robe and—only at that point—includes him at the party where there is held a feast. Those who have not received salvation have not accepted the invitation into the father's house. Those who (like the prodigal) accept the invitation receive both the robe of righteousness and the life-giving food and drink at the banquet of the Lord.

THE EXPERIENCE OF THE TABLE

The experience of the table, described in Revelation 3:20, is deeply personal and private. The *abiding relationship* has a personal dimension between ourselves and the Lord. However, the public ceremony of the Lord's Supper is corporate and modeled after the ceremony with fellow believers, which has been practiced for two thousand years. The Last Supper took place in the upper room, just before the arrest and trial of Jesus Christ. However, the private event at the table described here is to be done alone, within one's prayer closet. There can be no interruption. This personal time with our Lord should be safeguarded and done every day. The same prayer experience that Jesus shared with his Father may now be our privilege to share. The church sacrament of the Lord's Supper, corporately, does not take the place of our personal worship before God through the Son, our mediator.

This table experience is a celebration just as all marriage feasts may be. This time is for celebrating the power and love of God and our salvation and connection to Christ.

> *"Bring the fattened calf, kill it, and let us eat, and celebrate; for this, my son, was dead, and is alive again. He was lost, and is found." They began to celebrate (Luke 15:23- 24).*

The sacrament of the Lord's Supper is as a spiritual feast to nourish our faith, and to strengthen us to walk in all holiness by Christ living and working in us ... Its end is not only that we may remember Christ's death in the history, but in the mystery of it: as that His body was broken for us, that His blood is the blood of the New Testament, or covenant, shed for us, and for many, for the remission of sins, that so we may receive and enjoy all the promises of the new covenant which are recorded (Heb. 8:10-12). Its end is to mind us that Christ's body and blood are bread and drink, even all-sufficient food to nourish our souls to everlasting life; and that we ought to take, and eat, and drink Him by faith; and to assure us that, when we 'truly believe on Him, He is as really and closely united to us by His Spirit, as the food which we eat and drink is united to our bodies'. Christ Himself (John 6) does more fully explain this mystery–Walter Marshall.[15]

Being a relational experience like salvation, this celebration will involve exchanges back and forth. Neither a person nor the Lord can conduct this relationship alone. Both parties must participate. Jesus will initiate the exchange to which the disciple will respond. Jesus responds in turn—and so on.

THE ABIDING RELATIONSHIP
STEP ONE: *JESUS PRESENTS HIS SACRIFICE*

As they were eating, Jesus took bread, gave thanks for it, and broke it. He gave to the disciples, and said, "Take, eat; this is my body." He took the cup, gave thanks, and gave to them, saying, "All of you drink it, for this is my blood of the new covenant, which is poured out for many for the remission of sins (Matthew 26:26-28).

When we come to the table, Christ is already there waiting for us, for he cannot start without our presence. Much like the father of the prodigal, who waited for his son to come home, Christ waits. When we don't show up, both parties lose. This exchange relies upon our partnership. Upon our arrival, Jesus presents his sacrifice, his body, and blood. His body is the sacrifice he gave so that we would not have to die.

Every day when we pray before God, we receive Christ's blood and body (metaphorically), our nourishment. Though the Last Supper happened once in history, the meal is available to us daily as our daily bread. This meal can be enjoyed by us, privately during our prayer and worship time, just as it is celebrated by the church corporately.

> *Most certainly, I tell you, if a person keeps my word, he will never see death (John 8:51).*

This passage refers to the death of the soul, not the body (Matthew 10:28). His blood is the sacrifice that he gave for our forgiveness, our cleansing. Through the *abiding relationship*, we receive this eternal life and forgiveness of sins.

> *Moreover, he sprinkled the tabernacle and all the vessels of the ministry in the same way with the blood. According to the law, nearly everything is cleansed with blood, and apart from shedding of blood there is no remission (Hebrews 9:21-22).*

The Jewish nation understood blood sacrifice very well, having experienced hundreds of years of sacrifices in the temple. "The wages of sin is death, but the free gift of God is eternal life in Christ Jesus our Lord" (Romans 6:23). His body and blood were sacrificed for our sake, which put an end to animal sacrifice when these were also being abolished in the Temple.

THE ABIDING RELATIONSHIP
STEP TWO: *WE RESPOND TO HIS SACRIFICE*

We sit with Jesus at the table of his sacrifice. His instructions to us are clear. We are to eat his body and drink his blood.

Jesus therefore said to them, "Most certainly I tell you, unless you eat the flesh of the Son of Man and drink his blood, you don't have life in yourselves. He who eats my flesh and drinks my blood has eternal life, and I will raise him up at the last day. For my flesh is food indeed, and my blood is drink indeed (John 6:53-55).

Jesus puts forth two reasons we should eat his body and drink his blood. These first three verses (John 6:53-55) give us the first reason. We will live with him forever in God's kingdom.

He who eats My flesh and drinks My blood abides in Me, and I in him. As the living Father sent Me and I live because of the Father, so he who eats Me, he also will live because of Me (John 6:56-57 NASB).

These next two verses (John 6:56-57) give the second reason. Because of eating this sacrifice, we will live and abide in him. The mystery of the gospel concerns the manner of mutual abiding so that we become one flesh with the bridegroom. As Jesus Christ is in the Father, so we will be in the Son, and he will be in us.

The instructions to eat his flesh and drink his blood are just as big a stumbling block for us now as they were at the time of Jesus' ministry. The idea seemed very strange. Upon hearing these words, many of his disciples turned away and left. So many left that Jesus questions whether the twelve apostles will also leave. Peter answered for the group. They love him too much. Even without totally understanding his meaning, these disciples know that Jesus is the promised Savior who has the words of eternal life. A core group will stay with Jesus no matter what.

> *At this, many of his disciples went back, and walked no more with him. Jesus said therefore to the twelve, "You don't also want to go away, do you?" Simon Peter answered him, "Lord, to whom would we go? You have the words of eternal life. We have come to believe and know that you are the Christ, the Son of the living God" (John 6:66-69).*

The act of communion, whereby we eat the flesh of Jesus and drink his blood, brings about spiritual formation through the *abiding relationship*.

> *The essence of spiritual formation is precisely this: fostering the capacity, the orientation, the discipline of living in union with Christ–Gordon T. Smith.*[16]

The following topics show ways we can become one with him by eating his body and drinking his blood. The list, which is neither complete nor exhaustive, can be used as a starting point for worship. Individual approaches will vary and will change as our union with Christ becomes more complete. The points that follow are presented in a linear format. As these steps are practiced, they will become non-linear. An all-encompassing worship experience ensues. The *abiding relationship* unfolds.

1. REMEMBER

The act of remembering is vital for the *abiding relationship*. In contemplating who Christ is and what God has done through Christ, remember how Christ has saved, guided, and blessed us in the past.

> *Just as Christ died once and for all, so we are baptized and justified once and for all. Both events are in the strictest sense unrepeatable. Only repeatable is the recollection of the event that happened for our sake once and for all, and it needs to be repeated daily–Dietrich Bonhoeffer.*[17]

Such remembering is in accord with Christ's instructions to "do this in memory of me" (Luke 22:19).

> *Praise Yahweh, my soul, and don't forget all his benefits (Psalm 103:2).*

The Lord knows that we can be forgetful. The Old Testament has many poems and songs to help God's people remember his greatness and love. The table experience of dining with Jesus helps us to remember.

2. READ THE BIBLE

> *Every Scripture is God-breathed and profitable for teaching, for reproof, for correction, and for instruction in righteousness, that the man of God may be complete, thoroughly equipped for every good work (2 Timothy 3:16-17).*

Read the Bible, the word of God, to know God. The Holy Spirit will guide us into all truth. A specific and organized plan for reading is not as important as the sincerity of our intention. We should read to know God. We read from the heart not merely for knowledge. At the table, we eat the bread of the Lord, in whatever is provided, each day, and offered to us as wisdom. We drink the cup of divine love each day, too, uplifting the heart.

3. MEMORIZE SCRIPTURE

I have hidden your word in my heart that I might not sin against you (Psalm 119:11).

It is fascinating that memorizing scripture can be a tool for preventing sin. How mysterious are the ways of God? There are no set verses to memorize, for the Holy Spirit will show each one of us the verses to ponder and keep. These memorized verses will then become ours forever, which we may call on at any time. We shall know them so intimately that we will call on them even in the dark.

4. READ OTHER SPIRITUAL WORKS

God's people are still inspired by God, and some write and speak to inspire others. We should read some of these works, but we should also be careful about what we read:

Beloved, don't believe every spirit, but test the spirits, whether they are of God, because many false prophets have gone out into the world (1 John 4:1)

The Lord wants us to trust in the Spirit to be our guide, regardless of what we are reading. This trust is strengthened when we test ideas that seem to be out of accord with God's Holy Spirit of love. We ought to read and pray with discernment.

5. PRAY

Speaking to God is as natural as breathing. Even though the Spirit of God is mighty and infinite, God comes close to us in prayer. Our prayer should be like talking to an intimate friend. He is not in the faraway distant heavens. God is very close, even inside of us. Prayer is a unique exchange, individualized for each person, which will not proceed according to a fixed standard. The methods and means of prayer change as we grow closer to God in the *abiding relationship*. We don't even know the words to use or how to pray; the Spirit knows our hearts and the heart of God. The Spirit aids us in our prayer.

> *In the same way, the Spirit also helps our weaknesses, for we don't know how to pray as we ought. But the Spirit himself makes intercession for us with groanings which can't be uttered. He who searches the hearts knows what is on the Spirit's mind, because he makes intercession for the saints according to God (Romans 8:26-27).*

We ought to feel at liberty to tell God what is on our heart. Let us also listen to what he has to say.

6. CONTEMPLATE HIS GLORY

> *But we all, with unveiled face seeing the glory of the Lord as in a mirror, are transformed into the same image from glory to glory, even as from the Lord, the Spirit (2 Corinthians 3:18).*

Beholding the glory of God is the centerpiece of our contemplation. He must reveal himself to us so that we may recognize the divine glory. The traits of God are beyond our knowledge or understanding. His power, knowledge, patience, holiness, and mercy are beyond our reach or our thought. The Lord must show us what we could not grasp on our own.

Moses had walked closely with God for months before asking to see the divine glory. God then agreed to show Moses this divine goodness. God uses these two words interchangeably: goodness and glory. He put Moses in the cleft of a rock to protect him while he passed by and let Moses, his servant, only look at his back. While passing by the cleft, God proclaimed:

> *Yahweh! Yahweh, a merciful and gracious God, slow to anger, and abundant in loving kindness and truth, keeping loving kindness for thousands, forgiving iniquity and disobedience and sin; and that will by no means clear the guilty (Exodus 34:6-7).*

The glories of God, which we are to behold, are worth contemplating. Hebrews explains:

> *Therefore, holy brothers, partakers of a heavenly calling, "consider" the Apostle and High Priest of our confession, Jesus (Hebrews 3:1).*

7. CONSIDER HIS CREATIVE POWER

The creative power of God is revealed throughout the entire Bible. There are many references to this power. The psalmist loved God's creation.

The heavens declare the glory of God. The expanse shows his handiwork. Day after day they pour out speech, and night after night they display knowledge. There is no speech nor language, where their voice is not heard (Psalm 19:1-3).

More than any other visible image, God's creation reflects God's glory: the totality of the earth, seas, skies, and the entire universe. The beauty, majesty, and grandeur of God's glory through creation are overwhelming. The created world, exposed for all of us, shows who God is.

For the invisible things of him since the creation of the world are clearly seen, being perceived through the things that are made, even his everlasting power and divinity (Romans 1:20).

There is more spiritual richness in a single living thing or piece of nature than in a thousand sermons. We may contemplate a bird chirping, eating, flying, building a nest, or raising its young. What a magnificent and compact creature! Have humans invented anything even remotely close to the beauty and sustainability of a bird? Or close to any of the other creatures made by God's hand?

Shout for joy to Yahweh, all you lands! Serve Yahweh with gladness. Come before his presence with singing. Know that Yahweh, he is God. It is he who has made us, and we are his. We are his people, and the sheep of his pasture (Psalm 100:1-3).

8. PRAISE

Sing to Yahweh a new song! Sing to Yahweh, all the earth. Sing to Yahweh! Bless his name! Proclaim his salvation from day to day! Declare his glory among the nations, his marvelous works among all the peoples (Psalm 96:1-3).

We will be glad to lift our voices in praise since God is almighty. Let us praise the Lord from our hearts. Praise takes place between each individual and the Creator. The psalmist knew how to praise. Read the book of the Psalms. These hymns, the records of the psalmist's testimonies of praise, show us how to do likewise. We can sing praises in the songs that others have written. Sing aloud! Each one of us may collect the lyrics of favorite songs and read them, or sing and meditate upon them. These song lyrics record the sentiments of the composers who gave praise in their own ways. We can make the same praise songs our own. Or we may create our own songs of praise. Our new life itself will become a song of praise to God.

9. CONFESS AND REPENT

Have mercy on me, God, according to your loving kindness. According to the multitude of your tender mercies, blot out my transgressions. Wash me thoroughly from my iniquity. Cleanse me from my sin. For I know my transgressions. My sin is constantly before me (Psalm 51:1-3).

During moments of confession and repentance, we have time to recognize and acknowledge the sin in our lives. The Holy Spirit will bring our sins to mind. This particular task does not belong to us. We do not know what our sins are unless revealed to us by the Holy Spirit. The Lord is changing our lives, day by day, and yet we still fall short of where he wants us to be. Given our human imperfections, these failings are normal. We may expect to be contrite.

The Lord is a gentle, omniscient shepherd.

If our wrongdoing looms large in our minds, we may acknowledge our remorse without holding back and confess to the Lord our feelings. We acknowledge our inability to get rid of our faults. We must let God use the divine power, which we lack. Also, at times we know that we have done wrong, but we do not wish to change. We are all stubborn. In the Old Testament stubbornness is described as "stiff-necked." The Lord can work with stubbornness also if we will put it on the table. Let us acknowledge our failings together with our incapacity. We may share with God our pain and our remorse. Though we cannot do the work of change, the Holy Spirit will change our hearts.

> *Don't be afraid, little flock, for it is your Father's good pleasure to give you the Kingdom (Luke 12:32).*

THE ABIDING RELATIONSHIP
STEP THREE: *WE OFFER OUR SACRIFICE*

It may sound strange to refer to a new covenant of sacrifice. The old sacrificial system, which started after the fall of Adam and Eve, lasted up to the time of the cross. However, our Savior was the last blood sacrifice. No more blood sacrifices are required. The sacrifice we offer today under the New Covenant is a different kind. Not a sacrifice of blood nor for forgiveness, our sacrifice is a self-sacrifice, a giving of ourselves to our Lord. We are giving up the self-directed life and asking for the God-directed life. In self-sacrifice, a person falls on the rock and is broken to pieces. Yet, these broken pieces are collected and put back together again:

> *You also, as living stones, are built up as a spiritual house, to be a holy priesthood, to offer up spiritual sacrifices, acceptable to God through Jesus Christ (1 Peter 2:5).*

As disciples of Christ, we belong to a holy priesthood. Our daily sacrifices comprise the only spiritual sacrifice of which we are capable: ourselves. Our Lord receives our sacrifice once offered. Just as his sacrifice was voluntary, so is ours. We place ourselves on the table daily. We make ourselves available each day and recommit ourselves to God.

> *Therefore, I urge you, brothers, by the mercies of God, to present your bodies a living sacrifice, holy, acceptable to God, which is your spiritual service (Romans 12:1).*

> *Because the days of animal sacrifices are over, many people assume that all sacrifices offered to God are abhorrent to Him. That is simply not true. Here the apostle Paul calls for a new kind of sacrifice, a living sacrifice of our bodies. We are to give to God not our grains or our animals, but ourselves–R.C. Sproul.*[18]

Our sacrifice is a living sacrifice. Rather than sacrificing our will, we make use of it for our offering. Our will resides in the operational center of our mind. Since our unique personality remains intact and our identity (who we are) does not disappear, God incorporates his value system and his presence into us. In joining our spirit with God, the Spirit of God comes to occupy us more and more, so that we more fully reflect the divine glory. We are slowly restored to the image of God. The psalmist knew the correct sacrifice pleasing to God.

For you don't delight in sacrifice, or else I would give it. You have no pleasure in burnt offering. The sacrifices of God are a broken spirit. A broken and contrite heart, O God, you will not despise (Psalm 51:16-17).

This scripture tells how to give up the self:

Even so now present your members as servants to righteousness for sanctification (Romans 6:19).

Yes, we become servants to God, but only by our own choice. The apostles referred to their status as bondservants, who serve the Lord gladly, thankful that their debts had been paid. Christ redeemed us from our slavery to sin. Only two choices exist as to whom to serve. We can be voluntary servants of Christ, joining our spirit to the Holy Spirit, or we may be locked by chains of slavery to our own self-serving motives. While putting all of ourselves on the table—heart, mind, spirit—we rest upon the rock. Our sacrifice is now on the table. We wait for his response.

THE ABIDING RELATIONSHIP
STEP FOUR: *HIS RESPONSE TO OUR SACRIFICE*

After having acknowledged his sacrifice, and having placed our own sacrifice on the table, we now allow God to take his turn in our relationship. God's response, for which we wait eagerly, cannot take place without our cooperation (explained in steps two and three). Our relationship with God is a partnership. The individual places heart and spirit on the table. Empty of self, each person can now be filled, like vessels, by the Father's love.

And hope doesn't disappoint us, because God's love has been poured out into our hearts through the Holy Spirit who was given to us (Romans 5:5).

This love, the fulfillment of the law, is put into our hearts and absorbed by our minds (Hebrews 10:16). Because God is love, the spirit and being of Christ will fill our hearts and minds. As our rapport with God grows, the union between our Lord and us deepens. "He must increase and I must decrease" (John 3:30).

This "mystery of godliness" (1 Timothy 3:16) means that we are to obtain a heart of flesh, as one flesh with our bridegroom. The more complete our union with Christ, the more of God's being is inside us. Our *abiding relationship* may be characterized by these words: "Christ in you, the hope of glory" (Colossians 1:27).

Christ hosts this meal, and each time we meet him at the table, we choose again to rejoice in him, to bring our sorrows again before the throne of grace, to once more delight in his good gifts and to receive afresh the deep hope without which we cannot live. And then Christ feeds us – he gives us his very self, through the gracious power of the Holy Spirit, to go in peace, in joy and with courage into a fallen and broken world–Gordon T. Smith.[19]

This complete fulfillment, whereby Christ becomes one with us, does not happen at once. The process is slow and takes place gradually. The process will not be finished in our lifetime but will begin again in God's kingdom. During this process, something wonderful happens, as we become more and more at one with him. As we abide in him, we bear fruit.

I am the vine, you are the branches; he who abides in Me and I in him, he bears much fruit, for apart from Me you can do nothing (John 15:5 NASB).

But the fruit of the Spirit is love, joy, peace, patience, kindness, goodness, faith (Galatians 5:22).

We bear this fruit not because we pursue or even ask for it but naturally, through abiding. A growing tree bears fruit automatically, as a natural function of its growth.

The fruit of the Spirit is a gift of God, and only he can produce it. They who bear it know as little about it as the tree knows of its fruit. They know only the power of him on whom their life depends. There is no room for boasting here, but only for an ever more intimate union with him. The saints are unconscious of the fruit they bear–Dietrich Bonhoeffer.[20]

Union with Christ may be a long process just as fruit ripens gradually. The yield may be thirtyfold, sixtyfold, or a hundredfold. During the table experience, which is the highlight of the *abiding relationship*, we will have new and unique experiences. The Spirit is our guide. Our experiences will spill out of our prayer closet into our lives.

CHAPTER 6

GETTING CLOSER TO GOD: THE CLEANSING RELATIONSHIP

In this chapter, we will discover a third relationship, the *cleansing relationship*, which is an essential part of the sanctification process. The *abiding relationship* gradually fills our hearts with his presence and light. But there are parts of our hearts that prevent the light from filling it in full. Jesus calls these obstructions to light the "dark parts" (Luke 11:36). The *cleansing relationship* removes these dark parts. As with the first two relationships, this one requires our complete participation.

The *saving relationship* and the *abiding relationship* are glorious to consider. It is especially uplifting when we can truly participate and receive their life-giving benefits through the living water which springs up within us.

> *Whoever drinks of the water that I will give him will never thirst again; but the water that I will give him will become in him a well of water springing up to eternal life (John 4:14).*

In the first, the *saving relationship*, we become married to the bridegroom. Our branch becomes connected to the vine. We have life. In the second, the *abiding relationship*, our branch grows and bears fruit as we become united with our Lord. We are being changed by God through Jesus. Our hearts are filling with light.

As wonderful as these experiences are, the Lord has more good things in store for those that "hunger and thirst after righteousness" (Matthew 5:6). The third experience we may have with our Lord is the *cleansing relationship*.

The *abiding relationship* and its associated fruit-bearing cannot begin until the *saving relationship* is completed and we have become connected to the vine. Likewise, the *cleansing relationship* cannot begin until God sees evidence that our spirit is joining with Christ's Spirit. When our "branch" bears fruit, we are ready to cooperate with Christ in this third relationship, through the process of sanctification.

> *Every branch that bears fruit, he prunes, that it may bear more fruit (John 15:2).*

We must expand beyond the first two relationships, which are not enough for accomplishing all that our Lord has for us during our journey of union with him.

The *saving relationship* should be remembered every day. Although a vital part of our spiritual lives, the actual experience of being saved is short-lived. Nevertheless, the crucial connection made by being saved is necessary before we can begin to abide. The memory of this saving moment will help us stay focused on our Lord. The *abiding relationship*, which starts once we are connected to the vine, unfolds as a crucial part of becoming one with Jesus. The *abiding relationship* takes place in our private moments and in our prayer closets.

Just as our life is more than our private moments of worship, so the *cleansing relationship* begins once we leave our prayer closets. In the *cleansing relationship*, we walk with Jesus while interacting with others and engaging in daily business. When life's problems are getting us down, Jesus uses our real-time experiences in life as the stuff and raw materials for our progress so that we may be made whole. Our problems become opportunities once they are brought before God. We are relieved of undue anxiety, pain, and suffering.

THE CLEANSING EXPERIENCE OF PETER

The apostle Peter's life exhibits this stage of our discipleship. Peter, having been connected to the vine and having borne fruit, underwent a cleansing experience on the night of the arrest of Jesus.

God's people owe Peter a great debt. Perhaps more than any of the other followers of Jesus, Peter displays his humanity. Since we are all full of imperfections, including difficulties and problems, we can easily relate to Peter. Despite his shortcomings, his passion for the Lord is also obvious. Peter is like that exuberant student who speaks first in class, confident of having all the answers. He is always first to try something new, to express his opinion boldly, and to live with great passion—never deterred when he turns out to be wrong or to have failed. The group of apostles around Jesus was young. Just twenty-five years old (or so), Peter elicited several pointed rebukes from the Lord for his brash behavior. Thus, we can learn from both the positive and the negative traits of Peter–if we have ears to hear.

At the Last Supper and during the arrest of Jesus, Peter received four rebukes. The first occurred in the upper room when Christ was about to wash Peter's feet after having washed the feet of the other disciples. Peter refused this service, feeling himself to be unworthy, and it pained him to watch his master do such a menial task. Jesus told him, "If I don't wash you, you have no part with me" (John 13:8). After the foot-washing, as Jesus spoke about his death, Peter cried out that he would lay down his life for Jesus. Since Peter did not want his Lord to die, he planned to do everything in his power to prevent it. The Lord rebuked him a second time: "The rooster won't crow until you have denied me three times" (John 13:37).

After the Last Supper, Jesus and his disciples made their way to the Mount of Olives where it was their custom to spend the night in the garden of Gethsemane. Jesus felt the weight of sin settle upon his chest. His Father, who had been such a powerful companion, started to withdraw. Jesus separated from the group—by a "stone's throw," to pray. Peter, James, and John were "to stay here and watch with me" (Matthew 26:38). While Jesus prayed, the three men fell asleep. When he returned to check on them after an hour, Jesus rebuked Peter for a third time: "What, couldn't you watch with me for one hour?" (Matthew 26:40).

The last of Peter's rebukes occurred during the arrest of Jesus. This event had to be intimidating, even terrifying, for the apostles. Peter furiously drew a sword to defend his Lord. In doing so, he cut off the ear of the high priest's servant (John 18:10). Peter fell short for the fourth time. While healing the ear of the wounded man, the Lord rebuked Peter for striking out violently with his sword.

After his arrest, Jesus was taken into custody at the home of the high priest and interrogated. John and Peter, having followed the procession, were allowed into the building. Peter stood at the side of the courtyard by the fire with the servants so he could keep warm. As the measures against Jesus proceeded, the servants at the fire recognized Peter. They accused him three times of being a disciple of Jesus, and three times Peter denied his Lord.

The rooster crowed. Recognizing this sign, Jesus looked Peter's way. Peter remembered the meaning of the sign of the crowing. As he looked toward Jesus, their eyes met. Devastated at his downfall in all of its horror, Peter experienced the intimacy of the *cleansing relationship*. His Lord knew him too well; Peter had done exactly what he had vowed not to do, just as Jesus had predicted.

Peter had faced four trials by that night, and he had failed all of them. Having been rebuked four times by his Savior, whom he had wanted so much to please, he must have been plagued by an overwhelming realization of his own failure. He had disappointed Jesus and added to his Lord's burden that evening, instead of relieving it. Leaving that place, Peter found a secluded spot and "wept bitterly" (Luke 22:62).

The story of Peter, on the night of Jesus' arrest, is a saga of trial, failure, and rebuke. Peter's testimony, difficult as it may be, is similar to our own. All who follow the path of Jesus experience trial, failure, and rebuke. The *cleansing relationship* includes these experiences, though they may be unforeseen, which fall along the "paths of righteousness" (Psalm 23:3).

Peter's cleansing experience constitutes a vital component of his restoration. Disciples of Christ experience cleansing also, which is a vital part of our restoration. Through the *cleansing relationship*, our Lord restores us to righteousness—only according to our free consent, with our knowledge and participation. By taking part in this cleansing, we join forces with Christ. Our shortcomings may be recognized and removed. Peter could finally acknowledge the problem that the Lord had been trying to expose. Thus, he and his

Lord could address the matter together.

God creates victory out of failure when we acknowledge our weakness so that we may have access to divine strength. If this were not so, we would be tempted to believe that our own strength could change and sustain us. Yet, we are likely to be demolished by relying only upon ourselves. "Everyone who falls on that stone will be broken to pieces, but it will crush whomever it falls on to dust" (Luke 20:18). All power comes from God "for apart from me, you can do nothing" (John 15:5).

Peter fell on the stone that night, and he was "broken into pieces." He finally admitted his problem, caused by pride, arrogance, and self-reliance. He finally realized he had a problem in his life when there was nothing he could do to help himself. He could not change his bad behavior, no matter how hard he tried. Similarly, the apostle Paul recognized his own weakness:

> *There was given to me a thorn in the flesh, a messenger of Satan to torment me, that I should not be exalted excessively. Concerning this thing, I begged the Lord three times that it might depart from me. He has said to me, "My grace is sufficient for you, for my power is made perfect in weakness." Most gladly therefore I will rather glory in my weaknesses, that the power of Christ may rest on me. Therefore I take pleasure in weaknesses, in injuries, in necessities, in persecutions, in distresses, for Christ's sake. For when I am weak, then am I strong (2 Corinthians 12:7-9).*

We may claim the power of Christ when we are weak. The psalmist also knew the value of having his sins exposed through trials. Such is the path toward the righteousness of God.

> *Search me, God, and know my heart. Try me, and know my thoughts. See if there is any wicked way in me, and lead me in the everlasting way (Psalm 139:23-24).*

The psalmist prayed for trials that would expose his sin. Paul "took pleasure" in persecutions and distresses for the same reason. We are invited to embrace—like Peter, Paul, and David—our Lord in a *cleansing relationship*.

THE CLEANSING RELATIONSHIP

The *cleansing relationship* is illustrated by the same scripture we considered in discussing the first two relationships. In the counsel given to the Laodiceans (Revelation 3:18), eye salve is mentioned as the last of three items that the people of this church are to buy. The details of this symbol are described more fully in the very next verse (Revelation 3:19).

> *I counsel you to buy from me gold refined by fire, that you may become rich; and white garments, that you may clothe yourself, and that the shame of your nakedness may not be revealed; and eye salve to anoint your eyes, that you may see (Revelation 3:18).*
>
> *As many as I love, I reprove and chasten. Be zealous therefore, and repent (Revelation 3:19).*

The elements of the *cleansing relationship* must include:

- Eye salve for improved sight (v. 18)
- A statement of God's love for His people (v. 19)
- The experience of being reproved and chastened (v. 19)

These elements will all uniquely fit into this third relationship:

the *cleansing relationship*. While quite different from the first two, this relationship is essential to our lives so that we may be changed into the image of God. None of these three relationships is more important than the others for they all must be part of our life with God. This relationship is reciprocal and mutual, comprising four steps:

1. We fall short of the glory of God.
2. The Holy Spirit shows us our problem.
3. We see our problem; we acknowledge it and repent.
4. The Lord cleanses us.

These four steps reveal the same cooperation that has characterized the previous relationships. The *abiding relationship* is established in the prayer closet. Jesus invites us to go into our "inner room and shut the door" (Matthew 6:6) for a wonderful time of communion and sharing. While this experience happens daily, it is not meant to be a full-time occupation. We must be about our Father's business outside of our prayer closet. At that time, we take up our cross to follow Jesus Christ. The *cleansing relationship* happens during our walk with the Lord.

THE WALK

We do not follow Jesus to the cross. The Lord invites us to the cross. After the cross, we then follow Jesus.

> *He called the multitude to himself with his disciples, and said to them, "Whoever wants to come after me, let him deny himself, and take up his cross, and follow me" (Mark 8:34).*

First, we come, and then we follow. This sequence involves steps on the path which is called the "narrow way" (Matthew 7:14). This path has been walked by millions before us, all the way back to the times before the flood. Noah and Enoch, righteous heroes of old, both walked along this way. After each private table experience, the Lord will show us this path as well.

Righteousness goes before him, And prepares the way for his steps (Psalm 85:13).

A highway will be there, a road, and it will be called The Holy Way. The unclean shall not pass over it, but it will be for those who walk in the Way (Isaiah 35:8).

Each day, God gives us the same charge so we may know how we are supposed to act.

You are the light of the world. A city located on a hill can't be hidden. Neither do you light a lamp, and put it under a measuring basket, but on a stand; and it shines to all who are in the house. Even so, let your light shine before men; that they may see your good works, and glorify your Father who is in heaven (Matthew 5:14-16).

Walk as children of light (Ephesians 5:8).

These verses describe our daily mission and how we are to behave on the path which constitutes the narrow way. Early on as we walk in the steps of Jesus, we discover our many problems. The troubles in this world trip us up. Though Jesus says his "yoke is easy and his burden is light" (Matthew 11:30), he does not mean to diminish our problems. Jesus does not protect us from the earthly problems that everyone must face. Rather, the saying about the yoke and our light burden refers to the impact of sin and guilt on our lives. The responsibility for sin—and our guilt—has been lifted from us. Jesus has taken away our burden. Otherwise, we could not "walk in the paths of righteousness" (Psalm 23:3). Nor could we even find "where the good way is" (Jeremiah 6:16). While walking the path, tribulations will be present.

> *In the world ye shall have tribulation: but be of good cheer; I have overcome the world (John 16:33).*

These tribulations become the catalyst for our next level of righteousness. Our trials expose our hearts and our thoughts—not as punishment but as a component of our walk in and toward greater righteousness. We cannot take part in the growth of righteousness unless we know our failures, as Peter did on the night of the arrest. Our failures may then be relieved.

THE CLEANSING RELATIONSHIP
STEP ONE: *FALLING SHORT OF THE GLORY OF GOD*

What would we do without trials and tribulations? Life would not be life as we know it. Problems are intrinsic to life, just as accomplishments are. At times, troubles can be so intense that it may seem as if everything and everyone were conspiring against us. Yet, this hopeless feeling is so common that it must be considered normal. Neither one's wealth, fame, or power–nor even one's standing before God—will shield one from difficulties. At all ages and in all phases of life, problems are the stuff of our human experience in this world.

The Bible describes these problems as trials and tribulations.

Tests, trials, and temptations, in the New Testament, have specific spiritual connotations. For God's people who walk according to the Spirit, our tribulations become tests and trials. Such tests and trials are not intended to prove or to expose what is bad in our lives, nor are they meant for God to punish or reject us. These tests and trials are to expose and prove what is good, just as factory testing of a product proves its value to prospective buyers.

Job was tested by hardships. Abraham was tested when God asked him to sacrifice his son, Isaac. God allows *all* his people to be tested. This testing is not to prove that they are bad or they deserve punishment. Rather, God allows these tests so we may show forth and reflect his divine glory. All people experience trials. His people are no exception. We do not get a free pass from trials because we are his followers. His people of the light handle these trials differently from those who are not in the light. God is on trial with us and through us. We are walking in his power. We are the light of the world.

> *But we all, with unveiled face seeing the glory of the Lord as in a mirror, are transformed into the same image from glory to glory, even as from the Lord, the Spirit (2 Corinthians 3:18).*

God already knows our hearts. Our trials are not for his education. Instead, our trials are to educate the world that they may see God's glory reflected in us as we face the same difficulties as everyone else. A gospel scripture explains the purpose of good works: "That they might see your good works and glorify the Father which is in heaven" (Matthew 5:14). In this way, God draws others to himself. Our witness to others is about who we are and how we live. Our reflection of God's love and righteousness shows the world God's true nature. Our behavior is instinctive. We often remain unaware of its influence on others.

Temptation, unlike trials or tribulations, has a negative spiritual implication. The Greek word for both trial and temptation is the same (peirazó.3985). The translation depends on the context in which it is used. The word "trial" is used when there is a positive result. The word "temptation" is used when there is a negative result. The writer James captures the use of "temptation" perfectly in the following text.

> *Let no man say when he is tempted, "I am tempted by God," for God can't be tempted by evil, and he himself tempts no one. But each one is tempted when he is drawn away by his own lust, and enticed (James 1:13-14).*

Temptation signifies a failure of our hearts. According to the letter of James, temptation often involves lust or desire. The wrong desires of our heart turn a trial into a temptation. We "fall short of the glory of God" (Romans 3:23). Such was Peter's experience on the night of the arrest of Jesus. Pride, arrogance, and self-direction were products of the desires in Peter's heart. He wanted to be in control of Christ's mission, to have things his way, and to demonstrate that he knew best. However, Peter fell short of the glory of God, just as all of us who "walk in His ways" will do.

As we grow more and more complete in our union with the Lord, we can reflect his glory to a greater degree. In living our lives, we will *all* fall short of the glory of God. Even so, we remain connected to the vine. Our failures show us that we are not fully united with God. God uses these failures to bring us closer to him as he did with Peter.

Becoming one with God through Jesus Christ is gradual. He knows our progress, where we are on this pathway, and when we step off the path. His desire is not to condemn us or punish us, but to get us back on track.

> *Though the Lord may give you the bread of adversity and the water of affliction, yet your teachers won't be hidden any more, but your eyes will see your teachers; and when you turn to the right hand, and when you turn to the left, your ears will hear a voice behind you, saying, "This is the way. Walk in it" (Isaiah 30:20-21).*

On the night of the arrest of Jesus, Peter faced a trial. He was tempted and fell short of the glory of God. He stepped off the path. The Lord wanted to help him get up and get back on track. When we fall, the Lord does not condemn us. He wants us to get up, get back on the path, and walk again. He wants us to be closer to him.

THE CLEANSING RELATIONSHIP
STEP TWO: *GOD SHOWS HIS PEOPLE WHERE THEY FALL SHORT*

> *As many as I love, I reprove and chasten. Be zealous therefore, and repent (Revelation 3:19).*

The core principle of the *cleansing relationship* stems from the realization that we cannot repent and be cleansed until we recognize our shortcomings. We cannot see our shortcomings until they are brought to our minds by the Holy Spirit. We cannot have this experience until we bear fruit. And we cannot bear fruit until we abide in Christ and Christ in us.

Every branch that bears fruit, he prunes, that it may bear more fruit (John 15:2).

This pruning can only happen to branches that have borne fruit. The cleansing removes that part of our branch that is not bearing fruit. Only after we bear fruit can we see the portions of our branch that are fruitless. The problems in our lives become visible because the Holy Spirit shows them to us. Through this experience, the Lord eliminates the obstacles that stand in the way of a closer union with him and our fruitfulness.

At the moment when their eyes meet at Jesus' trial, there is no condemnation from Jesus to Peter. Only love resides in the eyes of our Lord. From looking into Jesus's eyes, Peter can remember that Christ knew his failure even before it happened. Peter remembers that Jesus had already prayed to the Father about his salvation. The Lord had already predicted both Peter's failure and his recovery.

The Lord said, "Simon, Simon, behold, Satan asked to have you, that he might sift you as wheat, but I prayed for you, that your faith wouldn't fail. You, when once you have turned again, establish your brothers" (Luke 22:32).

Since Jesus is on Peter's side, Peter is supported in coming through this cleansing experience successfully. Note the use of a double name in this address, "Simon, Simon," which is a token of endearment. While reproving his beloved disciples, Jesus sometimes makes use of a double name address. Martha was corrected with a double name address (Luke 10:42). Paul was corrected with the use of a repeated name during his conversion experience (Acts

9:4). Although Jesus knew that Peter would fail this test, he did not want Peter's faith to fail. Christ did not condemn Peter for he never condemns his followers. This reproof contributed to Peter's spiritual growth. Hence, he reproves Peter with the double name address. Similarly, Christ wants us to grow when we fall short.

In John 8:3-11, Jesus treats the woman caught in adultery much the same way. This woman may very well have been a disciple of Jesus. She calls him "Lord." He speaks to her as if she were a disciple. After scolding and removing her accusers, Jesus shows her the way back onto the path of righteousness—without condemnation.

> *Jesus, standing up, saw her and said, "Woman, where are your accusers? Did no one condemn you?" She said, "No one, Lord." Jesus said, "Neither do I condemn you. Go your way. From now on, sin no more" (John 8:10-11).*

Peter and this unnamed woman both needed to see the failure in their lives. If we don't know our failures, we cannot work with our Lord in their removal. He covers our sin during the *saving relationship*, but he cannot remove sin from our lives without our knowledge and participation; our free will is safeguarded. Our participation with God, in removing the sin that dwells within us, takes place in the *cleansing relationship*. We are all Peter. We are all the woman caught in adultery. Each of us needs to see and acknowledge our heart problems when Jesus shows us where we fall short. Jesus works on our sin problem at the heart level, not the action or surface level. When our heart is where he wants it, our errant behavior will disappear. Our behavior always follows what is in our heart.

The Lord's discipline is not at all like our own when we reprove our children, spouse, friends, or co-workers. In our world, when we are upset, we demand not only that people address and rectify their mistakes but that they also acknowledge that we are affronted. They must correct "their" fault, and their behavior, so that we may regain our good feeling and be relieved of being upset. Such self-concern is at the basis of our rebukes of others in our lives. Yet, this human manner of disciplining others is not the divine way.

Since Jesus knows the condition of our hearts, he is not surprised when we fall short. He is gentle and wants us to come closer to God through our experience of failure. Rather than walking away from Christ, we come to recognize our shortcomings while knowing we cannot fix them. Our Lord's rebuke shines a light into our hearts. Jesus is that light.

> *Again, therefore, Jesus spoke to them, saying, "I am the light of the world. He who follows me will not walk in the darkness, but will have the light of life" (John 8:12).*

Jesus shines the divine light into us to expose the lingering dark parts of our hearts. The darkness forms an obstruction to sanctification and to a closer union with him.

> *The lamp of the body is the eye. Therefore, when your eye is good, your whole body is also full of light; but when it is evil, your body also is full of darkness. Therefore see whether the light that is in you isn't darkness. If therefore your whole body is full of light, having no part dark, it will be wholly full of light, as when the lamp with its bright shining gives you light" (Luke 11:34-36).*

In this verse, Jesus demonstrates the use of eye salve (Revelation 3:18) to make our eyes "good." When our eyes are good, our whole body is also full of light. The eye salve is for our eyes to be good so that the divine light may shine into every corner of our lives. Our body is to be entirely full of light, without dark spots or areas. Remember the prayer of the psalmist regarding these cleansing benefits:

Search me, God, and know my heart. Try me, and know my thoughts. See if there is any wicked way in me, and lead me in the everlasting way (Psalm 139:23-24).

This divine discipline is a theme in Hebrews 12:4-11. Discipline from our heavenly Father is worthwhile and even a treasure. We have all been corrected, chastened, and reproved by our parents while they were responsible for us. All parents should correct the children they were privileged to raise. Hebrews indicates that we should expect the same from God, for our Lord treats us as his children. God only disciplines and chastises those whom he loves. Thus, discipline affiliates us to God as our Father. Without such discipline, we would be illegitimate in God's household. The Lord disciplines us for our own benefit so that "we may be partakers of his holiness" (Hebrews 12:10). Holiness is the outcome of sanctification by the *cleansing relationship*.

Spiritual discipline is not pleasant. Neither Peter at the trial of Jesus nor the unnamed woman caught in adultery took pleasure in having their sins exposed. This discipline is often difficult to experience.

All chastening seems for the present to be not joyous but grievous; yet afterward it yields the peaceful fruit of righteousness to those who have been exercised thereby (Hebrews 12:11).

Discipline does not make us feel comfortable, but the outcome of discipline is the "peaceful fruit of righteousness." Tears may flow; these are signs of repentance. Peter weeps. The woman caught in adultery repents, and Jesus does not condemn her. If we are disappointed at having fallen short of the Lord's righteousness, we show our devotion and our willingness to be cleansed. The reproof we receive from our Lord is always consistent with the message of Isaiah 30:21. God shows us that we have stepped off the path. He is close by to help us get up and return to walk on the path again. There is no condemnation from God.

THE CLEANSING RELATIONSHIP
STEP THREE: *WE SEE OUR FAILURES AND REPENT*

All the apostles and disciples received reproofs during their walk with Jesus, including Nicodemus, Martha, and the Samaritan woman (at the well). Reproofs occurred even after the resurrection and were directed at Thomas, Peter, the apostles collectively, and Cleopas with his friend (on the road to Emmaus). Today it is the job of the Holy Spirit to point out the failures of the disciples of Christ. If we have ears to "hear" and eyes to "see," it will be our privilege and honor to be reproved by our Lord. Thereby, we are loved and come into closer union with God. Here are some of the reproofs that Jesus gave to his beloved disciples during his ministry on earth:

- You are slow of heart to believe (Luke 24:25)
- Is your heart still hardened? (Mark 8:17)
- Why are you afraid? (Matthew 8:26)
- Oh, ye of little faith! (Mark 4:40)

- Why do you doubt? (Matthew 14:31)
- Do you still not understand? (Matthew 15:16)

As we have earlier discussed, Peter received four reproofs on the evening of the arrest of Jesus (or five if we count the unspoken reproof after his denial of the Lord). He did not hear the first four reproofs. Since his heart and mind were consumed by his fears regarding the Savior's own death, he could not receive correction himself. Self-oriented desires kept him from hearing earlier reproofs. Peter believed that the death of Jesus had to be stopped, and he wanted things to be his way. Once he publicly denied being a disciple of Jesus, Peter finally had eyes to see the darkness in his own heart. His sin had to become public to be visible to Peter. His mistake, which Jesus had predicted, exploded, and he "fell on the rock," weeping bitterly.

We are all Peter. Jesus waits for us to pay attention to his warning and his correction once we have stepped off the path. He is waiting for us to see the light, which is illuminating our hearts, to expose and drive out lingering dark spots.

After receiving our reproof, we must acknowledge our error and repent. Forgiveness is given by God's grace. Although we ask forgiveness for our problematic actions, we may ignore the conditions that are at their root. Peter's denial is rooted in the desires of his heart.

> *The good man out of the good treasure of his heart brings out that which is good, and the evil man out of the evil treasure of his heart brings out that which is evil, for out of the abundance of the heart, his mouth speaks (Luke 6:45).*

While we may sometimes exert our willpower to control our

actions, sin may remain within us. Willpower is of no value in removing sin or for changing our values. The work of Jesus, through the mystery of the gospel, cleanses our hearts, thoroughly and radically. It is a privilege to acknowledge the errors in our life that are shown to us by the work of the Holy Spirit. God's grace depends on our free will and voluntary cooperation. Without our consent and participation, our darkness will grow even stronger.

> *Jesus said, "I came into this world for judgment, that those who don't see may see; and that those who see may become blind." Those of the Pharisees who were with him heard these things, and said to him, "Are we also blind?" Jesus said to them, "If you were blind, you would have no sin; but now you say, 'We see.' Therefore your sin remains (John 9:39-41).*

In responding to God's discipline, we may be receptive—with tears of repentance—or obstinate. A model of obstinacy is provided by the story of the garden of Eden. When Adam and Eve were reproved in the garden, they tried to shift the blame. Adam pointed to Eve, and Eve pointed to the serpent. They both claimed before God that their wrongdoing was another's fault.

We have *all* justified our wrong behaviors in this manner. Besides shifting the blame, we can also deny that our behavior is sin at all—or again, we may deny that we have committed the sin. Peter offered such a denial and failed to respond to reproof. Adults and children may blame others or deny their responsibility when confronted with their disobedience—even when they are caught in the act.

To cooperate with our Lord in the *cleansing relationship*, our role is to acknowledge that we are completely responsible for our condition, without harboring secrets. Then, we can tell our Lord how we feel about our sin and repent. We must admit our own incapacity to remove the darkness inside. Thereby, we "fall on the rock." Because of the Lord's eye salve, which is forthcoming, our eyes become healthy. Then, our denial falls away. We can see.

We then take our hearts to put before the Lamb, who is Christ, on the table. Our sin becomes our sacrifice: a "broken spirit, and a broken and contrite heart" (Psalm 51:17). Grace, not willpower, will be strong enough to mysteriously change us from the inside out. If we can look deep enough into ourselves (in our private moments), we may not even want to change nor can we do so. However, if we realize our own resistance, this resistance may be sacrificed as well. Our hearts are on the table. We have repented. Our part is done. It is now the Lord's turn to take the final step with us to complete the *cleansing relationship*.

THE CLEANSING RELATIONSHIP
STEP FOUR: *GOD CLEANSES US*

Everything is ready for the final step. We have seen and acknowledged our sin. We have committed ourselves to God anew. We await the Holy Spirit, the indwelling power, which cleanses our hearts. Now we do nothing except wait upon God. Throughout our sanctification by faith, we allow the Holy Spirit to work in us. As a result, we are not infused by a super-strong willpower, as if to inoculate us from our tendency toward bad behavior. Sanctification is not a kind of penance by which to "fix" ourselves (supposing that fixing were even possible). Instead, our hearts are changed by God and our desires purified.

This process may take a few days, during which the Spirit may bring our faults to our mind again so we may recommit to the path of righteousness. This is not by a magic wand, nor is it an instantaneous process. We are being gradually purged. The dark spots are being removed from our heart. Our spirits are being restored since we have now allowed our spirit to join more closely with God's Spirit. This process is serious and, at times, severe. The Spirit may ask that we acknowledge and renounce our sin more than once. Nothing may remain hidden. Whenever we acknowledge wrongdoing in our lives, we are "anointing our eyes with eye salve." More light will shine through our eyes, banishing darkness throughout, so we may be "full of light." Through partnership, we become close to our Lord.

Occasionally, we may not want a particular darkness to be banished. We may feel justified in our resistance. At such moments, we should behave much like the desperate father who came to Jesus with his son.

Immediately the father of the child cried out with tears, "I believe. Help my unbelief" (Mark 9:24).

Soon, our resistance will melt; the dark spots in our hearts will dissolve. Several experiences over time may be required. The Lord will not let us experience more pain than we can bear, for God knows that we are fragile. He is gentle. Changes take time.

Peter needed patience but went on to become victorious. The Lord told Peter, "You, when once you have turned again, establish your brothers" (Luke 22:32). He did recover, and he did establish his brothers. He became a powerful and thoughtful leader for the new Christian era. Peter's sermon was used to convert the hearts of the men of Jerusalem on the day of Pentecost (Acts 2:14-36). Peter was used by the Lord to heal the lame man at the temple at the

Beautiful Gate. Peter went on to preach a second sermon, because of which he and John were both arrested. They spent the night in prison. Facing the Jewish rulers the next day, Peter spoke to the tribunal with confidence and power. Even the Jewish leaders knew this eloquence came from God (Acts 3:1-4:22). When arrested by Herod, Peter was rescued from a likely death by an angel. Releasing Peter from his chains, the angel escorted him out of the prison by night (Acts 12:1-10).

After these difficult experiences, Peter remained on a path of healing and cleansing. Even after his reproof and his denial of Jesus, he still fell short. After the resurrection, Jesus met the apostles in Galilee. He prepared food on the beach while some of his disciples had gone fishing all night. They all met on the beach and talked. Jesus told Peter how he would die. Peter then asked about the future death of the beloved disciple. Jesus answered him, "If I desire that he stay until I come, what is that to you? You follow me" (John 21:22).

Even twenty years later, when Peter met and ate with Paul and a group of Gentile Christians, Peter still fell short, once again. After the Jewish Christians from Jerusalem arrived, Peter separated himself from the Gentiles. He would share table fellowship only with the Jewish Christians from Jerusalem. Peter condoned an improper prejudice against the Gentiles within the Jewish community—for which Paul reprimanded Peter publicly (Galatians 2:11-14). The Lord used Paul as his instrument. Peter was still growing. So was Paul. A continual cleansing process occurs in the life of all believers. Position, status, or even holiness do not exempt one from this ongoing work of the Spirit.

Sanctification resulting from the *abiding relationship* occurs as

Jesus comes into our lives more fully each day. This table experience can be thought of as sanctification by "addition." God's Spirit is being "added" to our spirit. Sanctification as part of the *cleansing relationship* can be thought of as "subtraction." Once the "dark parts" (Luke 11:36) are "subtracted" from our hearts, there is room for God's Spirit, which is light:

> *Your body gets its light through your eyes. When you have good eyes, all your body has light. But when your eyes are bad, your body is in darkness. So be sure that it is not dark in you where it should be light. If no part of your body is dark, it will all be light. It will be like a lamp that shines to give you light (Luke 11:34-36).*

TESTING AND TRIAL WITHOUT FAILURE

The *cleansing relationship* is about cooperating with our Lord to clean the darkness out of our hearts. Yet, not all trials become temptations. As we walk with Jesus day-by-day, we become more united with God. The divine thoughts and desires become our own. Trials are never eliminated, and we continue to face them each day. How we face these trials varies as we are directed by the Spirit. Our trials become our Lord's trials, and his trials become our own.

> *But you are those who have continued with me in my trials. I confer on you a kingdom, even as my Father conferred on me (Luke 22:28-29).*

As we pass through trials while the Lord's strength is working through us, we reflect the glory of God to the world. Our light shines bright, reflecting the bright light which is God. We experience trials the way the Lord intends us. As Jesus came through trials with the Father working through him, we are to come through trials likewise.

> *It is to the glory of God that we be fully and completely who we were created to be—Gordon T. Smith.*[21]

A different method of sanctification is experienced as we come through trials as the Lord intends.

> *Consider it all joy, my brethren, when you encounter various trials, knowing that the testing of your faith produces endurance. And let endurance have its perfect result, so that you may be perfect and complete, lacking in nothing (James 1:2-4 NASB).*

James seems to be the expert at addressing trials. In this verse, he explains that our tests produce endurance. Endurance, in turn, results in our being "perfect and complete, lacking in nothing."

Sanctification is more than a relational experience. It is a supernatural event and a mystery. Sanctification flows as naturally as a vine bearing fruit. As a result of our union with Christ, we grow into the likeness of God's image. God is working through us. Our behavior is instinctive. It happens without our planning or thinking.

James writes of the joy we experience as we face various trials. Joy is one fruit of the spirit. To experience joy during trials may seem impossible for human beings, but for God nothing is impossible. In walking with Jesus, we may not always feel victorious.

> *Just as the separation of Church and world became visible only in their continuous conflict, so also does personal sanctification consist in the conflict of the Spirit against*

> *the flesh. The saints are only conscious of the strife and distress, the weakness and sin in their lives; and the further they advance in holiness, the more they feel they are fighting a losing battle and dying in the flesh–Dietrich Bonhoeffer.*[22]

The passage describes what the letter of Timothy might call fighting "the good fight of faith" (1 Timothy 6:12). This effort, which postpones gratification until our resurrection, requires patient endurance. Jesus, while living on earth, endured until the end. So must we.

> *For we were saved in hope, but hope that is seen is not hope. For who hopes for that which he sees? But if we hope for that which we don't see, we wait for it with patience (Romans 8:24-25).*

No power on earth can bring us through life victoriously, except the love of God and love from God. God called us, and we came to him. Jesus asked us to follow him, and we followed. We give our hearts to God, and he gives us divine love. He is our God, and we are his people. In this way, the people of God multiply. Abraham and Moses walked in this way, as did the apostles and the early Christians.

These three relationships describe the process of coming to God so that we may be part of his people: the *saving relationship*, the *abiding relationship*, and the *cleansing relationship*. The pathway of righteousness and sanctification is the good way, which leads to the restoration of the soul.

CHAPTER 7

SOME PEOPLE JUST DON'T WANT TO FIND GOD

The three relationships with God, which we have discussed, outline how we may come to God and how we stay connected to him and in his grace. These relationships show us our role when walking the paths of righteousness. Through them, God remakes us into his image. The references to these three relationships are spread throughout the Bible from Genesis to Revelation.

Revelation 1–3 contains messages to the seven churches in Asia. The seven messages announce that the churches of Jesus Christ are to persevere unto the end. The trials we face on this earth require endurance. Jesus loves the churches and wants them to be in God's kingdom. He calls out each church for any wrongdoing in their midst. The seven churches are also provided counsel in these chapters regarding how to overcome their problems.

The last of the seven churches is uniquely different from the others. While all six churches have gone astray, the perils facing the seventh church are described in more detail and greater specificity. The advice to the church of Laodicea in Rev. 3:18-20 contains the three solutions to finding God: the *saving relationship*, the *abiding relationship*, and the *cleansing relationship*.

In substance, each of these three relationships is separately explained throughout the Bible in many passages. This short passage in Revelation, however, summarizes all three together as a package. Although Jesus directs each of the seven messages to a particular church, respectively, each church is asked to hear and understand all the messages for all the seven churches, collectively. The messages are for us, too. The seventh letter details how we may walk in the paths of righteousness.

The city of Laodicea was wealthy. Located on one of the major east-west highways through Asia Minor, the city was situated at the crossroads of lucrative trading opportunities. A city of industry, it possessed its own medical center. The city was equipped with a piped water supply system, which transported water from miles away. Laodicea must have been among the most modern and prosperous cities of the region. Four references to the Laodiceans are made in Apostle Paul's New Testament letter to the Colossians (Colossians 2:1; 4:13, 15, 16). Colossae and Laodicea were only ten miles apart.

The Christian church at Laodicea must have been wealthy as well. However, this church also had its problems. One of the accusations against the Laodicean church in Revelation 3 is that its members boast, "I am rich, and increased with goods, and have need of nothing" (Rev. 3:17). God does not agree with their self-evaluation. He advises otherwise: "They were wretched and miserable and poor and blind and naked" (Revelation 3:17).

These Laodiceans were in a bad place and were not aware of their condition. While much can be learned about the Laodicean church in Asia Minor, there are important questions we might consider as we read about these early Christians. What is in the hearts of these people? What are their desires? Who do they represent? Is there a lesson here for us today?

A historical analysis of this region does not tell us why this group received the particular warnings and counsel in Revelation 3. The most important fact about the people of this ancient church is that they represent a type of believer which exists in many other times and places, even today. Like the parables of Jesus, the Laodiceans are symbolic figures, timeless, who represent a particular spiritual attitude and a particular problem. Although the message of Revelation is full of riddles, there are identifying marks that clearly characterize the group. The message is not unlike what we can find in the parables of Jesus and in parts of the Old Testament.

The characteristics of the Laodiceans are clear. First, the Laodiceans are church members. Joined to Jesus in a *saving relationship*, they are saved (in modern parlance). That the Laodiceans are church members is essential to grasping the significance of the message to the seventh church in these chapters. The messages for all seven churches of Revelation are for the disciples of Jesus, for people who have connected themselves to Jesus Christ. Jesus would like his followers to stay connected with God through him and to become one with him. There is more to experience after salvation—indeed, the fullness of life.

Based on their works, the Laodiceans are lukewarm, neither hot nor cold. The Laodiceans are stuck. They cannot experience growth as Jesus desires. Yet they will not walk away from Jesus, either. They were in a middle zone. The Lord makes it clear that their works are at issue, and he knows their works. Our actions reveal our character and our hearts.

A similar message is directed to the people of Capernaum in John 6:

Don't work for the food which perishes, but for the food which remains to eternal life, which the Son of Man will give to you (John 6:27).

Although the people of Capernaum immediately wish to know what they must do to accomplish the works of God, they dislike the answer.

They asked him, 'What works does God ask us to do?' Jesus answered them, 'The work that God asks you to do is to believe in the one whom he has sent.' (John 6:28-29).

Like the people of Capernaum, the Laodiceans were not doing the works of God. They were not allowing the Savior to change their hearts. The Laodiceans were resisting this change. They did not think it necessary.

Another quality of the Laodiceans is that they suppose themselves to be self-sufficient and in need of no help. They have many goods with little need for anything more. The perceived wealth or self-sufficiency of the Laodiceans poses a common spiritual problem in the early church, one that still exists today.

The Laodiceans are also in trouble because of ignorance. They are unaware of their true condition: wretched, miserable, poor, blind, and naked. This last problem of ignorance may be the most pernicious and malignant. They are caught in a dilemma. They have ended up in a very poor condition because they have not listened to God. Stuck, they need help to remedy their predicament. Yet, they cannot get a remedy for their difficulty until they are able to listen to God.

These traits can be found in other stories, parables, and lessons related to the same condition throughout the Bible. Taken together, these lessons display in detail the problems that can beset followers of God and Christ after their salvation experience.

Every believer faces the problems of the Laodiceans to some extent. Each of us is responsible for listening and responding to the Holy Spirit about our lives. Family and friends may point out obvious, open, and public rebellion against God. The rebellion in our hearts, however, is subtle and not so overt; it can only be known by each of us in private. Most sin is internal, hidden in our hearts. The darkness in our hearts is always known by God. The Holy Spirit makes our problems known to us, but we will not know them unless we can "hear" his voice. Only by the Holy Spirit can we learn that we have a need when we believe that we require nothing.

The detailed advice to the Laodiceans in Revelation sets out paths of righteousness. The Lord gave the seventh church directions for the three paths of righteousness. Both for the Laodiceans and for God's people today, these paths assure that we can keep our first love. By repenting and doing the work of God, we take part in these three relationships, thus overcoming our spiritual problems. These paths establish the way to endure until the end.

This advice, as we showed earlier, is not only for the churches of Revelation but also for all of God's people past, present and future. His people are to be with him forever. Christ wept in pain over Jerusalem because the people of this city refused to be taken under the wings of the Almighty. Our Lord cries over everyone who rejects God, just as we cry when we are rejected by someone we love. Our God is the God of love.

God wants no one to remain unfruitful. While Jesus walked on earth, the Lord told parables of the Laodicean condition. Some people may be connected to the vine while remaining unfruitful.

They cannot abide in him. Like vines in need of pruning, they need the shears of the divine gardener.

The stories that follow were spoken by Jesus to explain this Laodicean type of problem. Jesus used analogies, metaphors, and parables.

THE SOWER AND THE SEED

The Parable of the Sower and the Seed offers a powerful simile of how people respond to God. Four types of responses are described, represented by four types of seeds and soil. The story may have been told frequently while Jesus and his disciples traveled by foot throughout the land of Israel. They went to the coast of the Mediterranean, as far north as Tyre and Sidon, to the east of the Sea of Galilee. They worked south from there, through Samaria, and down into the region of Jerusalem and Jericho.

Jesus and his disciples must have visited hundreds of villages, many of them more than once. Most were very small. Jesus likely told this Parable of the Sower in every town. The parable is well documented in three of the Gospels: Matt. 13:3-9, Mark 4:3-9, and Luke 8:5-8. The parables are similar in each of these three Gospels. The parable is given, together with an interpretation. The parable is first told as a story and shared with a public audience which had gathered to hear from this powerful prophet. The story could be subtle and hard to understand. For some of the listeners, its meaning would unfold later as they meditated upon the words. The Holy Spirit would open their hearts and minds to understanding.

After the parable was told openly, there was an interpretation shared with the disciples in a more private setting. His private listeners included not just the twelve apostles but all those who followed Jesus. Even some new followers may have listened to the interpretation. Those who already believed in Jesus as the Messiah could be taught with greater and more direct clarity. Jesus spoke plainly to them, expounding the terms of the parable, because they had "ears to hear."

Blessed are your eyes, for they see; and your ears, for they hear (Matthew 13:16).

For the three gospel versions of this parable, a supplementary interpretation was provided. Minor differences among the versions of the parable do not detract from the story; instead, they enhance it. As the story of each seed is related, pay particular attention to the roots and the fruits of each plant. Such metaphors are thematic throughout the Bible and provide keys for understanding the parable.

First Seed

And as he sowed, some seed fell by the road, and the birds came and devoured it (Mark 4:4).

This seed represents those who hear the message of God but neither understand nor want any part of it. It represents those who wonder why the message could mean so much to others. The teachings, which seem to be foolish, go in one ear and out the other—forgotten. As such, the first seed in the parable does not germinate. The seed has no root and bears no fruit for the listener.

Second Seed

Others fell on the rocky ground, where it had little soil, and immediately it sprang up, because it had no depth of soil. When the sun had risen, it was scorched; and because it had no root, it withered away (Mark 4:5-6).

The second seed represents those who hear the words of God's message and like it. This message makes sense to them because it has evidently produced good results in the lives of others. Such listeners long to experience beneficial results in their own life. They believe they are doing right by following the example of the true believers. The problem is that the heart of the second listener, who represents this second seed, is neither touched nor changed. They do not have the power of the Gospel. They only have a form of religion. This kind of person decides to become a disciple of Jesus because they want to do what others are doing. They wish to do what is popular. Such motivations are not lasting. The hearts of those that follow Jesus must be deeply changed. When this group of people meet adversities and persecutions common to Christians, they stumble. They disconnect themselves from the Christian community. In this parable, the second seed falls away; it withers.

The second seed germinates. The root extends downward but cannot connect to the soil below. Instead, the root stops in the rock layer and cannot receive the life-giving nutrients from the soil. This second seed, like the first, ends up with neither root nor fruit.

Third Seed

Others fell among the thorns, and the thorns grew up, and choked it, and it yielded no fruit (Mark 4:7).

The third seed represents the listener who hears the message of God and believes it. The heart is changed, and one becomes connected to Jesus. Accordingly, the root extends down into the soil level. Connected to the soil, the seed receives nourishment. This seed represents people who are in a *saving relationship* with God. They are joined to him.

The problems such listeners face differ greatly from those of the second seed. They occur after the root receives nourishment from the soil and the plant matures. As in the case of the second seed, the third seed faces the same problems of adversity and persecution. However, they overcome these trials successfully. The believer maintains a connection with God. The problem is different. Even though this kind of believer has come through affliction and persecution, he or she is choked by:

1. The cares of this world
2. The deceitfulness of riches
3. The lust for other things
4. The pleasures of this life (Mark 4:19)

These problems are referenced in the parable by the choking of the weeds. Because of this choking, the seed "brings no fruit to perfection" and it remains "unfruitful." It is important to note that this third seed is choked but does not lose its root. It is unfruitful, while maintaining its connection with the soil. The plant does not wither (as did the plant from the second seed). This third seed has a root, but no fruit.

Fourth Seed

Others fell into the good ground, and yielded fruit, growing up and increasing. Some produced thirty times, some sixty times, and some one hundred times as much (Mark 4:8).

This fourth seed is the true believer and the mature disciple. This seed is connected to the soil (as is the third seed). The fourth seed represents the person who has weathered the adversities and persecutions of the world, the same adversities that caused the second seed to wither. Here, the plant stays strong. As the fourth seed gives rise to a plant that grows and matures, the plant does not become choked with thorns. This seed produces fruit, "some thirtyfold, some sixtyfold, some a hundredfold."

You didn't choose me, but I chose you, and appointed you, that you should go and bear fruit, and that your fruit should remain (John 15:16).

This fourth seed has a root and produces fruit.

THIRD SEED PROBLEMS

The people represented by the third seed are in the same condition as the Laodiceans and match their characteristics. First, they are members of the church. Even though choked, the roots of the plant are still in the soil bringing life. They are not withered. However, they are lukewarm, just like the Laodiceans, neither hot nor cold. If they were hot, they would be comparable to the fourth seed. If they were cold, they would be compared to the second seed. They are lukewarm, instead.

The third characteristic that links the parable of the third seed to the situation of the Laodiceans pertains to riches. The Laodiceans believe they are rich. They have many goods without need of anything else. Yet, they are choked by the deceitfulness of riches. This deceitfulness of riches lies in the belief that worldly wealth is all that a person needs. They are satisfied with the riches they have.

The rich man in Luke 12:13-21 exhibits this problem. He tears down his barns to build bigger barns. This man, also like the believer represented by the third seed, loses sight of the spiritual wealth that our Lord wants to provide. The believer represented by the third seed is lacking in spiritual wealth. Thus, this kind of person is unfruitful and does not grow to maturity.

THE UNFRUITFUL SERVANT

The Parable of the Talents is found in two places: Matt. 25:14-30 and Luke 19:12-27. The details of the two stories vary somewhat, but their message is exactly the same. As we discussed earlier in this book, the last servant in this parable buries his gold in the ground and hides it. The original gold from his master has shown no increase. This servant feels no need for this increase and ignores instruction from his master. This servant then makes a weak excuse for his failure to profit. This last servant is like the Laodiceans; he felt he needed nothing further. His root is connected to the soil but bears no fruit.

> *For I tell you that to everyone who has, will more be given; but from him who doesn't have, even that which he has will be taken away from him (Luke 19:26).*

THE UNFRUITFUL TREE

Everyone loves trees. Trees are a marvelous part of our world. Some we plant and care for, but the vast majority seem to replant themselves and grow with no care on our part. All trees are beautiful, but fruit trees are a particular delight. They provide benefits to be appreciated with our eyes and our taste.

Fruit trees fulfill a major role in God's instruction to us about righteousness, starting in the Old Testament and continuing to the New.

Blessed is the man who trusts in Yahweh, and whose trust Yahweh is. For he shall be as a tree planted by the waters, who spreads out its roots by the river, and shall not fear when heat comes, but its leaf shall be green; and shall not be careful in the year of drought, neither shall cease from yielding fruit (Jeremiah 7:7-8).

Jesus speaks clearly in the New Testament about this fruit.

I am the vine. You are the branches. He who remains in me, and I in him, the same bears much fruit, for apart from me you can do nothing (John 15:5).

Jesus talked about fig trees frequently. The storyline and meaning were always the same. The fig trees were connected to the soil from which they received nourishment. These beautiful trees looked radiant and healthy like the other fig trees. However, the trees were unhealthy. As alluring as they looked, they bore no fruit. Their lush vegetation gave the promise of good fruit. This lack of fruit is evidence that the people represented by these trees are not abiding in Christ. The union of the Lord's Spirit with their spirits has not occurred. They still rely on their own wisdom and power.

They are connected to Jesus but lead a self-directed life. Those looking for fruit from these beautiful trees are repeatedly disappointed. These fruitless trees may be compared to the Laodiceans.

THE UNFRUITFUL BRIDES

In the parable of the ten virgins (Matthew 25:1-13), the oil represents the Holy Spirit. The Spirit is the instrument for uniting the Lord's Spirit with our own. All ten virgins await the bridegroom. They were all connected to the vine as disciples of Jesus Christ. The five foolish virgins do not see the need for the extra oil—for they need nothing. Nor do they abide with Christ or form a union with him. They ignored their poor standing before God. Like the third seed, they have a root but no fruit. They are comparable to the Laodiceans.

GOD DESIRES FOR EVERYONE TO CONNECT WITH HIM AND BEAR FRUIT

Since the garden of Eden, our God has always wanted his people to connect with him, to become one with him, and to bear fruit. This fruit is the mark of righteousness through union with God. God places righteousness in the hearts of his followers as he becomes one with them. The lessons represented by the third seed are for those people called by Christ toward radical discipleship. He desires them to follow him totally—all the way into a perfect union. This discipleship is the only way toward happiness and joy, so that we may be remade into God's image.

Christ loves these disciples and doesn't want to lose any of them. They have already shown that they have "ears to hear." They have already recognized his voice and joined him. But something is holding them back from bearing fruit. They are connected to the vine, but they are choked.

Once connected to Jesus, no one should be separated from him. Jesus longs for his people to accept the counsel of Revelation 3:18 and to obtain treasure in heaven. He desires to be in each of us so that we may be in him. He wants us to grow closer to him, to be joined with the vine, to grow into a perfect union with him and to bear fruit. He has given us these three wonderful relationships to become one with him:

- The *saving relationship*
- The *abiding relationship*
- The *cleansing relationship*

This volume is now complete. Each reader has the tools of participation with our Lord. He longs for each of us to be reconciled to God through him. He invites you to become completely one with the Father. It is our privilege that God desires his works to be done through us. Today is the day of salvation. Today is the best day to start. May you be filled with the fullness of God.

NOTES

1. W. Ian Thomas, "The First Man Adam." *The Mystery of Godliness: Experiencing Christ in Us,* Fort Washington, CLC Publications, 2014, 1110.

2. Gordon T. Smith, "Evangelism, Spiritual Practice and Spiritual Formation." *Called to be Saints: An Invitation to Christian Maturity*, Downers Grove, Intervarsity Press, 2014, 60.

3. Gordon T. Smith, "In Christ: The Essential Character of Christian Experience." *Called to be Saints: An Invitation to Christian Maturity*, Downers Grove, Intervarsity Press, 2014, 42.

4. Gordon T. Smith, "In Christ: The Essential Character of Christian Experience." Called *to be Saints: An Invitation to Christian Maturity*, Downers Grove, Intervarsity Press, 2014, 50.

5. R.C. Sproul, "Be Holy Because I am Holy." *The Holiness of God*, Carol Stream, Tyndale House Publishers, 1985, 167.

6. W. Ian Thomas, "The First Man Adam." *The Mystery of Godliness: Experiencing Christ in Us,* Fort Washington, CLC Publications, 2014, 1110.

7. W. Ian Thomas, "The Nature of the Mystery." *The Mystery of Godliness: Experiencing Christ in Us,* Fort Washington, CLC Publications, 2014, 541.

8. Walter Marshall, "The Duty of Believing." *The Gospel Mystery of Sanctification*, London, 1692, 53.

9. W. Ian Thomas, "The Nature of the Mystery." *The Mystery of Godliness: Experiencing Christ in Us,* Fort Washington, CLC Publications, 2014, 574.

10. Dietrich Bonhoeffer, "The Image of Christ." *The Cost of Discipleship*, New York, MacMillan Publishing Co., 1963, 338.

11. Dietrich Bonhoeffer, "The Saints." *The Cost of Discipleship*, New York, MacMillan Publishing Co., 1963, 320.

12. R.C. Sproul, "Be Holy Because I am Holy." *The Holiness of God*, Carol Stream, Tyndale House Publishers, 1985, 167.

13. W. Ian Thomas, "The Law of the Spirit of life." *The Mystery of Godliness: Experiencing Christ in Us,* Fort Washington, CLC Publications, 2014, 1779.

14. Gordon T. Smith, "Appendix A: Worship and the Formative Power of the Liturgy." *Called to be Saints: An Invitation to Christian Maturity*, Downers Grove, Intervarsity Press, 2014, 194.

15. Walter Marshall, "The Means of Holiness to be Used in Faith." *The Gospel Mystery of Sanctification*, London, 195.

16. Gordon T. Smith, "Evangelism, Spiritual Practice and Spiritual Formation." *Called to be Saints: An Invitation to Christian Maturity*, Downers Grove, Intervarsity Press, 2014, 58.

17. Dietrich Bonhoeffer, "The Saints." *The Cost of Discipleship*, New York, MacMillan Publishing Co., 1963, 311.

18. R.C. Sproul, "Be Holy Because I am Holy." *The Holiness of God*, Carol Stream, Tyndale House Publishers, 1985, 161.

19. Gordon T. Smith, "Union with Christ: Reprise." *Called to be Saints: An Invitation to Christian Maturity*, Downers Grove, Intervarsity Press, 2014, 180.

20. Dietrich Bonhoeffer, "The Saints." *The Cost of Discipleship*, New York, MacMillan Publishing Co., 1963, 320.

21. Gordon T. Smith, "Evangelism, Spiritual Practice and Spiritual Formation", *Called to be Saints: An Invitation to Christian Maturity*, Downers Grove, Intervarsity Press, 2014, 26.

22. Dietrich Bonhoeffer, "The Saints." *The Cost of Discipleship*, New York, MacMillan Publishing Co., 1963, 321.

www.ingramcontent.com/pod-product-compliance
Lightning Source LLC
Chambersburg PA
CBHW030326080526
44584CB00012B/727